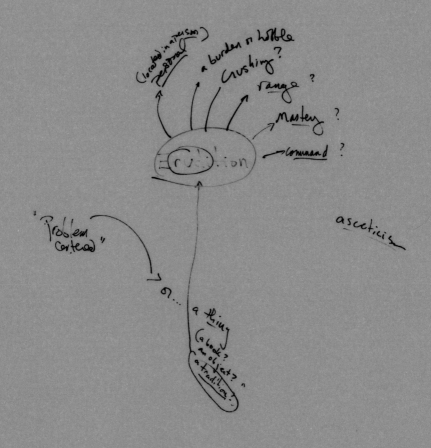

(located in a person)
personal

a burden or hobble

Crushing?

Erudition

range ?

Mastery ?

command ?

asceticism

"Problem centered"

or...

a thing
(a book?
an object?
a tradition?)

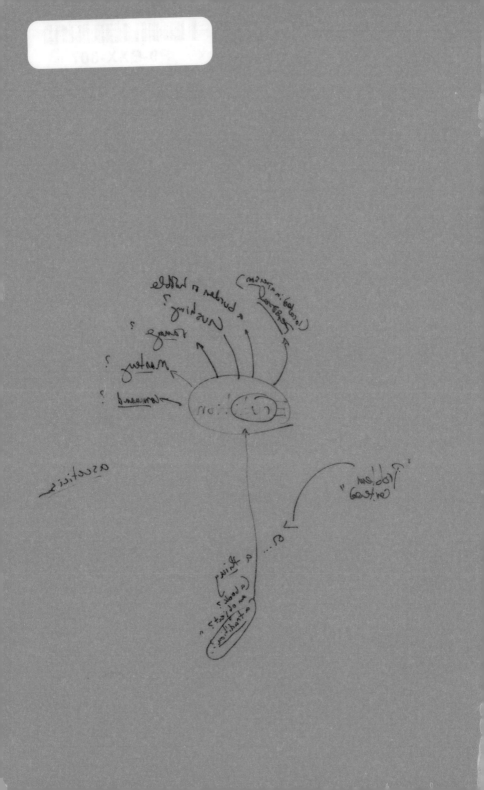

Object

	pure	impure
pure	pure pure	pure impure
impure	impure pure	**impure impure**

Method

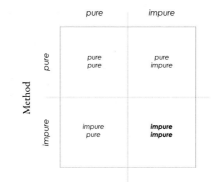

KEYWORDS;

FOR FURTHER CONSIDERATION

and

PARTICULARLY RELEVANT

to

ACADEMIC LIFE

Authored by

A COMMUNITY OF INQUIRY *

IHUM BOOKS

in association with

PRINCETON UNIVERSITY PRESS

MMXVIII

Published by
IHUM BOOKS
Interdisciplinary Doctoral Program in the Humanities at Princeton
Princeton University
Princeton, NJ 08544
princeton.edu/ihum

Distributed by
Princeton University Press
41 William Street
Princeton, NJ 08540
press.princeton.edu

Library of Congress Control Number: 2017958697
ISBN: 978-0-691-18183-7
British Library Cataloguing-in-Publication data is available

* The "Community of Inquiry" consisted of: Paul Baumgardner, D. Graham Burnett,
Kate Yeh Chiu, Jeff Dolven, Michael Faciejew, Thomas Matusiak, Candela Potente,
Matthew Rickard, Jessica Terekhov, and Enzo E. Vasquez Toral

Editors: D. Graham Burnett, Matthew Rickard, and Jessica Terekhov
Design: Kate Yeh Chiu

With special thanks to: Christie Henry, Brooke Holmes, Anne Savarese, the IHUM
Executive Committee, the Center for Collaborative History, and the Council of the
Humanities at Princeton University

This book has been composed in Garamond Premier Pro and Century Gothic

Printed in the United States of America

10 9 8 7 6 5 4 3 2 1

KEYWORDS

INTRODUCTION ix

INTRODUCTION

The present text took shape in the shadow (or is it the light?) of two presiding works of criticism that are disguised as glossaries: Raymond Williams's classic *Keywords: A Vocabulary of Culture and Society* (1976), and Ambrose Bierce's wicked *Devil's Dictionary* (1911). Strange bedfellows, to be sure. The Welsh Marxist gave the world a series of absorbing, studied essays on one hundred terms central to the analysis of social life and cultural production—bound together in a volume that condensed a career of sustained reflection on art, literature, and politics by one of the great progressive intellectuals of the twentieth century. By contrast, the bilious cynicism of Bierce, a hardened American journalist and wounded veteran of the Civil War, eventually found issue in a casual torrent of skewering *aperçus* concerning the vanity and vacuity of "modern" life—a roll call of zingers, many of which still sting. On the one hand, hopeful and generous learning. On the other, bitter and misanthropic satire.

For all the differences between these two books, each reflects the highly personal and idiosyncratic voice of its author. But the volume before you can claim no such unitary maker. And in that regard, a third glossary project must be mentioned here as an inspiration for the current undertaking: the "Collective Dictionary" project of the organization known as Campus in Camps, founded by Sandi Hilal and Alessandro Petti. Campus in Camps functions as a collaborative and politically engaged pedagogical project within the Dheisheh Refugee Camp in the West Bank of Palestine. As part of the ongoing work of bringing a shared awareness to generations of young people in that challenging environment, Hilal and Petti have, over the years, encouraged each campus "class" to contribute to the collective drafting and redrafting of a set of short essays on key terms shaping the lifeworld of Dheisheh. Words like "participation" and "ownership." Charged words, in context. And the work of reaching a shared understanding of that context is meant to happen in the course of the collaborative defining and redefining of those words.

Each of these three dictionary-like things has contributed something to the spirit of our project. From Williams, we have taken the serious proposition that our critical and productive possibilities are absolutely inextricable from the existence of a shared lexicon—that the richness of our discourse is a function of the richness of that lexicon, which to possess and activate we must attend to with live minds, historical sensitivity, and lots of questions. From Bierce, we have taken the liberating license of irony, together with a commitment to impiety wherever it may work its astringent virtues. From the utopian/emancipatory enterprise of Campus in Camps, we have taken the promising hope that collaborative work on the meanings of words can be a powerful way to build and strengthen communities, and prepare them to work for change.

And so what is this thing that we have made together, thusly inspired? And who were we?

In brief, *Keywords;...Relevant to Academic Life, &c.*
emerged out of a graduate seminar taught at Princeton
University in the spring term of 2017. The title of the
course was "Interdisciplinarity and Antidisciplinarity,"
and it convened under the auspices of the university's
Interdisciplinary Doctoral Program in the Humanities,
or IHUM, an initiative less than a decade old and aimed
at nurturing experimental and forward-looking Ph.D.-
level work across history, literature, philosophy, music,
architecture, and the other relevant domains of art and
learning. The course description read, in relevant part:

> Academic life is largely configured along
> disciplinary lines. What are "disciplines," and
> what does it mean to think, write, teach, and
> work within these socio-cognitive structures?
> Are there alternatives? This course, drawing
> on faculty associated with the Interdisciplinary
> Doctoral Program in the Humanities (IHUM),
> will take up these questions, in an effort to
> clarify the historical evolution and current
> configuration of intellectual activity within
> universities. Normative questions will detain us.
> The future will be a persistent preoccupation.

We were about ten students and faculty in regular
attendance, drawn from nearly as many departments.
Across the term, we received weekly visits from a
dozen distinguished scholars: Lucia Allais, Andrew
Cole, Devin Fore, Hal Foster, Eddie Glaude, Anthony
Grafton, Federico Marcon, Rachel Price, Eileen Reeves,
and others. Each assigned us a classic text from his or

her area of expertise—by request, a text that would be of use to us in our effort to understand both the enabling power and limiting perspectives of disciplinary inquiry. The resulting syllabus was arguably eclectic (though not especially "diverse": Althusser, Derrida, Du Bois, Eco, Husserl, Kluge, Momigliano, Warburg, etc.), but our conversations were surprisingly focused: again and again we came back to fundamental questions about humanistic inquiry—its ends, its means, its past, its present, and its prospects. And this meant a return, again and again, to the primary institution that has sheltered and nurtured humanists: the university.

A summary of the class is beyond the scope of this introduction (though we did draft such a document together over the term). Here it will suffice, perhaps, to say that the course toggled productively between two very different registers. From the outset, there was a strong inclination to ask a frighteningly general and deep question about our work as students and teachers: What is worth doing? What intellectual work is real and good (as opposed to merely "tactical" or "pragmatic" within the micro-arbitraging cosmology of *Homo academicus*)? If that line of inquiry represented the "high road" of aspiration and vision, we paired such moments of noble folly with a salutary return to the "low road" of nuts-and-bolts inquiry into the local ecology of higher education: we followed the money; we examined incentive structures; we were skeptical and (at least provisionally, heuristically) disabused of any residual idealisms. The result was, for many of us, both stimulating and clarifying. And if nothing else, the mood of the inquiry fostered a very real sense of shared enterprise.

This keywords project emerged in that context, as a final collaborative exercise. We collated about fifty terms that had come up across the semester in the course of our discussions, and that seemed central to our concerns. We divided them up. And we each (students and faculty) took on the task of drafting definitions (sly, dutiful, resistant, surreal, impassioned) that drew on and spoke to our conversations and readings over the semester. These individually drafted texts then spilled into a jointly-authored manuscript that underwent a summer of participatory expansion, editing, and consolidation. The book in your hands is the fruit of that labor. The decision to publish it under collective authorship was itself made collectively, and each contributor retained the option to pull his or her material out of the enterprise right up to the end. But an iterative project of writing and re-writing left us with texts that all were willing to treat as the work of all. Yes, to be sure, some worked more and some worked less. And yes, it is probably the case that no one of us feels that the totality of the work herein represents wholly congenial reflection. But it has been interesting to work to make a text that—in process, structure, and content—defies a number of the standard conventions of academic production. One should not overstate this. It is, after all, a perfectly recognizable product, this little volume. But still, we wrote it "together" and all elected to sublate our individual authorial voices in a collaborative text-project that cuts across students and faculty from several different departments and programs—and that is a little unusual.

There is no manifesto in these pages. And no "call to arms," exactly. But the reader will surely notice, here and there, the sharpness of a voice expressing discontent or frustration—and that voice at times resolves itself into something close to provocation. If one were to try to sum it up, this provocation, one might say that this text seems to ask, again and again, in different ways, whether the current configuration of the university serves the high ideals of the humanistic tradition. And whether we, the inheritors of that tradition, and its devotees, have yet been equal to the call. The text pushes: How could we do better?

And that vigorous dissatisfaction must rebound onto this volume itself, which thinks of itself as a first pass at the terrain it wishes to cover, and which looks to the future for correction, revision, and whatever extension might be deemed appropriate. Should such work ever be undertaken, we wish those who turn to it as invigorating an experience as it has been our pleasure to share.

KEYWORDS;

FOR FURTHER CONSIDERATION

and

PARTICULARLY RELEVANT

to

ACADEMIC LIFE

ACADEMIA

The institutions that collectively sponsor and promote research, generally in connection with programs, centers, and departments that administer undergraduate and graduate education; sometimes the professional organizations with which these activities are affiliated; less often, the private and semi-private corporations that contribute to this work. Used pejoratively (i.e., "academic"), the work of said institutions and their denizens insofar as it is difficult or obscure. The term comes by the latter associations honestly, deriving as it does from the grove outside Athens in which Plato delivered lectures. Plato's Academy was not a school, nor did it have a curriculum. The space was used for exercise in DIALECTIC. By its very nature, this pseudo-method of interrogation and exchange resists the definite conclusions that are required of ordinary tasks, and it inclines toward the speculative limits of philosophical inquiry. When the term returned to prominence in Renaissance Florence after a prolonged period of disuse, it described the flurry of activity being undertaken to recover the learning (or non-learning, as it were) of Ancient Greece. Academia expanded beyond humanistic scholarship in subsequent centuries—in that numerous elite cliques called themselves "academies" in order to describe their shared conception of intellectual endeavor in fields like vernacular writing (*Accademia Fiorentina*), artistic practice (*Akademie der Künste*), and scientific research (*Académie des Sciences*)—but the academies of the seventeenth and eighteenth centuries maintained the esoteric tradition they inherited from Florence and Athens. Alongside their productive research in mathematics, physics, and chemistry, academies sponsored work on magic, alchemy, astrology, and kabbalah. Interest in the hidden or the occult spanned the British, French, and Prussian Academies; practitioners in these domains included Isaac Newton and Gottfried Leibniz. All but the most fervent rationalists presumed that any understanding of the natural world would necessitate a *détente* with forces that no less sober a mind than David Hume called "obscure and uncertain." Academies were functionally absorbed by the modern research UNIVERSITY in the nineteenth century, and today academia is effectively indistinguishable from the university itself, in its full socio-cultural and pragmatic reach. The remaining independent academies are in fact populated by scholars essentially all of whom hold university posts. Thus the function of academia in its current form (if not always its explicitly stated mission) is that of the university in its modern configuration: service to the global economy through the production of monetizable knowledge, together with the rearing of students into desirable employees for profitable firms. The tensions with the original design of the "academy" are pronounced, though it is unclear to what extent this genealogical awkwardness imperils the enterprise. If critics no longer accuse academia of concealing a trove of hidden knowledge, they instead levy a charge that is all the more distressing for its banality: that academia is not *mysterious*, but *useless*.

AMATEUR

The enthusiastic lover of some domain; hence, for practical purposes, the opposite of an expert (see EXPERTISE). The expert is responsible to the protocols of a DISCIPLINE, wherein objects of study exist to realize methods for knowing them. The amateur is responsible to the object of study itself, if he/she is responsible at all. Of particular interest to interdisciplinary studies is a middle category: inquiry by a trained mind in a field for which the mind is untrained. This is the *amateurism of experts*, informed by the possibility of method, respectful of the achievements of scholarship, but helpless to reproduce the expected forms of knowledge.

A
B
C
D
E
F
G
H
I
J
K
L
M
N
O
P
Q
R
S
T
U
V
W
X
Y
Z

ART

Most generally, the ability, manner, or "knack" essential
to the realization of some task or goal, especially when
tricky or specialized; i.e., "the art of losing isn't hard
to master." Also, a large class of objects and/or non-
material phenomena privileged for their putative ability
to occasion unpredictable but significant responses
(particularly aesthetic, but sometimes sentimental or
political) in individuals and groups. A term substantially
defined by resistance to definition. Hence, difficult
to define satisfactorily, if also satisfactory to define
difficultly.

AUDIENCE

In general, the entity to which a communicative gesture—artistic, didactic, performative, or otherwise expressive—is addressed. (*Academic*) The subset of scholars who engage with specialized research on select topics, ideas, or categories through idiomatic conversation. (*Obsolete*) The universal public; the human community.

A
B
C
D
E
F
G
H
I
J
K
L
M
N
O
P
Q
R
S
T
U
V
W
X
Y
Z

BIBLIOGRAPHY

Etymologically, the writing of books; presently, the description or enumeration of books already written. As an appendage to academic scholarship, the bibliography can be said to offer a genealogy of an author's intellectual resources. The (generally alphabetical) bibliography of a scholarly work amounts to a constellation of adjacent and coincident texts; it situates the work itself within a (putatively) emergent field of interlocutors, even as it also (generally) invokes a more or less pregiven disciplinary territory. It is nevertheless rare that one encounters identical bibliographies for different works. Bibliographies thus resemble snowflakes, insofar as they elaborate a "uniqueness" (a mastery of texts that is ultimately bound to an individual scholar) that is from any distance perfectly monotonous. Though commonly understood as a "thing," bibliography also refers to the systematic description of books as material objects, sometimes, as in the case of cataloguing private collections, with attention to the correspondence between knowledge and its position in space. The architectural dimension of the bibliography reminds the reader that the text is not constituted as a stable knowledge-object, but is in fact rearticulated by its user. Thus the bibliography may reveal an author's omissions, secrets, and blind spots, no less than his/her considerable ERUDITION; indeed, it may reveal that the work fails to produce knowledge over and against the texts in the bibliography itself. In this case, the truest bibliographer would be the librarian, who pledges to care for knowledge rather than make it.

CANON

A sacred weapon within academic departments, fired
ritually upon the uninitiated or wayward. Injuries
suffered may generate the scars requisite for entry into the
relevant sodalities and/or encampments.

A
B
C
D
E
F
G
H
I
J
K
L
M
N
O
P
Q
R
S
T
U
V
W
X
Y
Z

CITATION

A reference within a TEXT, broadly conceived, to another text, also broadly conceived. The text may contain citations that vary by the degree to which they explain their own referentiality: from the explicit (such as quotation, footnote, endnote, or epigraph) to the implicit (such as paraphrase, allusion, imitation, or homage). Professions tend to require explicit citations for certifying specific claims; they may also encourage implicit citations to ensure that an author belongs to his/her community and shares its range of experience and interest. Within ACADEMIA, citations represent measures of pertinent evidence and access points to relevant information. Citations are increasingly used in the HUMANITIES (they have operated in this way in the sciences for some time) as quantifiable metrics of a scholar's significance: to be much cited is to *exist more* within a given discipline, or more thoroughly to have permeated its corporate body, in something of the way in which a dominant allele can be said to have achieved "prominence" in a given population. Standards of citation differ according to field, being enforced (without violence) by journals, presses, and professional organizations such as the Modern Language Association or the American Psychological Association. These norms thereby come to shape the identity of the scholar and of scholarship. By design, they indicate (and can even be said to constitute) the author's grasp of existing scholarship in his/her DISCIPLINE, and they encourage him/her to "advance" the body of knowledge involved. Such advancement, interestingly, tends to mean the de-citation, over time, of texts once understood to be obligatory citations within the discipline. In this way, the citation is a device whereby a scholar contributes to

the semi-autonomous and depersonalized progress of
knowledge itself (see KNOWLEDGE PRODUCTION).
And yet the citation also preserves the romantic ideal of
individual intellectual genius. The attempt to eliminate
ambiguity from the field of reference reinforces the
primacy of the author as such—this especially in the
humanities, where multi-author publications are scarce.
The whole phenomenon is perhaps best witnessed in the
culture industry. There, citation is ubiquitous, yet rarely
acknowledged. This is the case in visual media such as
television, film, and photography, in which the artist
cannot—or need not—rely on the quotation mark or like
device to distinguish borrowed from original material.
One might argue that such media call into question the
fixity of textual reference; or one might argue that they
reveal textual reference for what it is. For the culture
industry confronts "citation" in a narrow sense only at the
abstract and distant boundary of copyright infringement,
which requires an enormous amount of capital (in
addition to compelling argumentation) to litigate.
Within the triangular network of producer, consumer,
and commodity, the citation reverts to its ancestral form:
property.

A
B
C
D
E
F
G
H
I
J
K
L
M
N
O
P
Q
R
S
T
U
V
W
X
Y
Z

COMMITTEE

A corporate body, generally chartered or commissioned by some authority, and configured for the purpose of deliberation, regulation, and/or governance. Because colleges and universities tend, by TRADITION, to be run in a participatory-collaborative way (with substantial faculty and student involvement in policy management), committee-work represents a significant feature of life on campus—particularly for the faculty, one third of whose triumvirate of formal institutional obligations (teaching, research, and service) is largely discharged by sitting on committees. These committees often assemble in seminar rooms on campus, which circumstance probably informs the frequently musing, ruminative, and open-ended character of committee conversations in an academic setting.

CRITIQUE

As distinct from criticism, with which it ought not be confused. Criticism is the (often negative) appraisal of ART; critique is the (always negative) appraisal of criticism.

A
B
C
D
E
F
G
H
I
J
K
L
M
N
O
P
Q
R
S
T
U
V
W
X
Y
Z

DEPARTMENT

The smallest degree-granting unit into which
ACADEMIA has been partitioned, so as to advance the
knowledge of highly particular concerns. Whether the
department has been successful in this endeavor is, for
want of a department devoted to this question, difficult
to say.

DIALECTIC

A style of thought poised at such a remove from the
objects of its analysis that all difference turns out, upon
sufficient reflection, not to exist. With the obvious
exception of the difference between dialectic and
everything else.

A
B
C
D
E
F
G
H
I
J
K
L
M
N
O
P
Q
R
S
T
U
V
W
X
Y
Z

DICTIONARY

Any of a wide variety of lexicographical works, generally arranged alphabetically (or by the structural features of characters, in the case of logographical languages), and purporting to offer useful information about words— paradigmatically their meaning and usage, though also often their history, pronunciation, equivalents in other languages, etc. While word lists of various sorts can be found in many ancient literate traditions, the emergence of the dictionary as such correlates with the codification of national languages across the early modern period. Samuel Johnson, whose *Dictionary of the English Language* (1755) significantly shaped the language in which it was written, snuck a charmingly self-deprecating note into his magnum opus, describing the maker of a dictionaries as a "harmless drudge" immersed in quietly bookish labor. His rough contemporary Voltaire, however, composed a *Dictionnaire philosophique* (1764) that was intended as a cudgel for the descending of the *Ancien Régime*—and deployed to that end.

DISCIPLINE

A category of human knowledge constituted through
the sedimentation of objects, methods, bibliographies,
traditions, conversations, and debates—usually in an
institutional space (see DEPARTMENT). It is not without
reason that disciplines are commonly attributed to
the intellectual-historical transformations of the later
nineteenth century, which introduced the "modern
research university"—and, moreover, many of the
disciplines considered self-evident (and the disciplinary
arrangements taken for granted) today. The coincidence
of modern disciplinarity with early specialization
and professionalization is not, in fact, coincidental.
Disciplines, couched within universities, enabled the
accreditation of scholars destined neither for the habit of
the priesthood nor for the habitude of "men of letters"
(nor, for that matter, for remunerative careers in law or
medicine—as appealing then as now). The result was
the "professional academic," an individual committed to
KNOWLEDGE PRODUCTION within a given FIELD.

A
B
C
D
E
F
G
H
I
J
K
L
M
N
O
P
Q
R
S
T
U
V
W
X
Y
Z

DISCOURSE

The specialized linguistic corpus of a disciplinary or professional enterprise. Discourse designates the language practice of a scholarly or professional community, including a shared vocabulary, as well as a common tone or style. In this sense, discourse can be figured as the dialect or idiom of a given BIBLIOGRAPHY and the questions, issues, and topics it circumscribes. Discourse is the medium for conversation among members of a particular DISCIPLINE or PROFESSION. Literary discourse, then, exists alongside legal discourse, while macroscopic entities (e.g., the humanities at large), institutions (e.g., the United Nations), and conceptual categories (e.g., aesthetics) can also be discursive. Accordingly, discourses can be mutually intelligible and their terms, transferable; but discourses are nevertheless predicated on specificity insofar as they foster association and its obverse— exclusion. Within the academic setting (as in other socio-cognitive environments), a sense of disciplinary identity or "belonging" stipulates the existence of a community *outside* a given set of linguistic protocols, an "other" not privy to or fluent in the language of a certain intellectual conversation. As such, discourse represents a marker of distinction that serves a discriminating function across disciplines or among audiences for scholarship, despite the fact that varieties of discourse proliferate and ostensibly coincide. Membership in a disciplinary community requires a process of linguistic acculturation whereby a scholar becomes attuned to the relevant specialized registers of various words, phrases, concepts, or expressions—a dynamic rather incandescently on display in this very paragraph and elsewhere in the present volume.

EDUCATION

The course of study undertaken by an individual. Insofar
as it denotes the sense of "bringing up" or "rearing"
(generally young children or animals), education
refers more precisely to the path taken by a maturing
individual—a meaning evidenced in the etymology of the
word, which derives from the Latin *ducere*, "to lead" (with
the important prefix "e/ex," implying "out of"; suggesting
that such a path must be *out of* something—presumably
ignorance, though perhaps bliss). Such a foreshortened
and perhaps rather imprecise definition, if necessary,
nevertheless raises important questions. What objects of
study does education involve? If education is conducted,
does it presuppose direction or mentorship? And if
education is a progress, where does it lead? Education
takes the entire body of human knowledge as its point
of reference; it refers to the development of conceptual
understanding as well as applied skills, without restriction
to either intellectual labor or its alternatives, whatever the
putative distinction. This inclusivity among the objects
of study predicated by education extends to the agents
involved, who may be scholars, or skilled workers, or
entrepreneurs, or policy-makers, and so on. Education,
then, runs the gamut of pre-professional, vocational, or
occupational opportunities available to any individual—
or, at least, it should. Education fundamentally straddles
pedagogy (e.g., a degree in education certifies new
teachers) and knowledge acquisition (an education is
said to be "earned" or "obtained"). Education is thus
both imparted and received, whether interpersonally
or through texts or artifacts as proxies for instructors.
However, it instantly retreats from the universal to the
particular, from the communal to the individual, in

A
B
C
D
E
F
G
H
I
J
K
L
M
N
O
P
Q
R
S
T
U
V
W
X
Y
Z

its possessed state: hence, "*my* education," in whatever
field. When education designates the course of study
undertaken by an individual purely in pursuit of
knowledge of X, such that this knowledge becomes
the object and the objective of learning, he/she may
be said to have "become knowledgeable" about X. Yet
no such knowledge can be understood adequately to
encompass the embodied/subjective activity of "being
led to knowledge of X"; nor, it would seem, the equally
embodied/subjective business of "being in possession
of knowledge of X." It is possible that, where the
HUMANITIES are concerned, these latter dynamics and
conditions are particularly in need of elaboration, with
implications for education in that domain.

EMANCIPATION

Freedom; arguably the single highest political/
intellectual ideal across much of the world, at least in the
wake of late eighteenth-century developments commonly
referred to as "the Enlightenment." Many scholars in the
humanities and social sciences write books and articles
that seek to *emancipate* readers, generally from what are
understood to be ideological misprisions inimical to the
proper experience or full exercise of human freedom.
Interestingly, however, relatively few of the scholars in
question seem to have a robust account of into what
condition of existence it would be ideal for humans to be
freed. But this is a very hard problem. Gestural micro-
maneuvers away from one or another punitive non-
freedom will generally suffice in the introduction and/or
conclusion of a scholarly work.

A
B
C
D
E
F
G
H
I
J
K
L
M
N
O
P
Q
R
S
T
U
V
W
X
Y
Z

EPISTEMOLOGY

An intellectual enterprise formally concerned with
explaining how knowledge is possible. There are
two kinds of epistemology, strong and weak. Strong
epistemology begins by considering whether it is possible
to know anything at all. What is the relation between
SUBJECT and OBJECT, such that the one can know the
other? Weak epistemology assumes that knowledge is
possible, all too possible. How many ways of knowing can
there be, and what can they know about one another?
In the critical philosophy of Kant, the task is to define
the limits of reason, what it can know of the structure
of reality and what it cannot. In the anthropology of de
Castro, there is the jaguar and the human, the jaguar for
whom blood is beer, and the human for whom beer is
blood. The first kind of epistemology is the province of
the philosophers, and it is a condition for all work in any
DISCIPLINE, a conceptual deference owed by a thinker to
a given structure of EXPERIENCE. Its interdisciplinarity is
its universality. The second kind of epistemology can be
said to be dispersed among the disciplines, and each may
attempt to lay claim to its own. For the anthropologist,
blood is custom; for the historian, a clue; for the critic,
a word; for the jaguar, again, it is beer. How does the
jaguar know its beer? A difficult question, but to ask it
is to assume already that it does, that there is a discipline
of the jaguar, within which beer can be known and even,
somehow, said. There are weak epistemologies, which
assume that the disciplines of the jaguar and the historian
can never intersect. There are strong epistemologies,
which allow for translation and transformation, for the
critic to know the word as his beer as his blood, and for
the jaguar to crouch at the pool of her ink. Epistemology

may, on this field of contention, risk losing the last of its *a priori* authority, devolving into rival perspectives, or discourses, each seeking to remake the other in its own terms (see DISCOURSE). There are two kinds of epistemology, weak and strong.

A
B
C
D
E
F
G
H
I
J
K
L
M
N
O
P
Q
R
S
T
U
V
W
X
Y
Z

ERUDITION

Broadly, learning, especially in abundance. The term is generally used to refer to large amounts of knowledge, particularly of systematic (or at least coherent) form, particularly when it is in the possession of a human person, and readily accessible to that person. One could only awkwardly speak of a book "containing" erudition; the word carries with it, in ordinary usage, the implication of a conjunction of knower and knowledge, and, furthermore, tends to imply that the conjoint state is a felicitous one for the knowing subject (at least). It is interesting to note that the etymology of the word links it to the process whereby the rude or uneducated are led out of that condition—accordingly, brought to some measure of sophistication or polish. In this sense, the term would seem to have strong links to pedagogical traditions and the broader project of the formation of the youth in different cultural settings (see EDUCATION). At present, however, the term seems to have lost most or even all of these connotations, and is used almost exclusively to refer to a mass of learning in the possessed state, without reference to the process whereby it came to be possessed. For reasons that are obscure, the term seems to have little or no place in the physical or life sciences, and is closely linked to the domains of secular, text-based inquiry often grouped under the rubric of the HUMANITIES. It is tempting to suggest that the broad history of learned culture can be told as a dialectical (or zero-sum?) contestation between an *ésprit érudit*, on the one hand, and an *ésprit critique*, on the other (see DIALECTIC). The former embodies a program of proliferation, collation, and omniscient mastery; the latter, a program of excision, reduction, and foundational precedence. It is unclear if these respective enterprises are best thought of as mere tactical positions in the skirmish-spaces of intellectual conflict, deep characterological tendencies in the psychology of thinkers, or coherent strategies for advancing actual conceptions of what thought should do.

A
B
C
D
E
F
G
H
I
J
K
L
M
N
O
P
Q
R
S
T
U
V
W
X
Y
Z

EXCELLENCE

The substantive form of the familiar adjective "excellent," meaning "of the highest quality," and, more specifically, "surpassing related or adjacent members of the relevant class." As a noun, the term designates the state of being "better than" other persons, places, or things. Interestingly, while it permits the conveyance of this sense, the term never requires that the surpassing of the broader field be specified: from a grammatical perspective, the comparative or competitive implications of the word are sublimated. Excellence is the basic objective of most modern human activity in developed societies. Within the expansive culture of neoliberalism, excellence functions a little like money: everyone needs to pursue it; the pursuit of it is considered not only the pursuit of a fundamental good, but also a fundamentally good pursuit, one that has the capacity virtuously to organize and to motivate both individual and collective life. Within academic settings, the pursuit of excellence—by persons and institutions—is essentially the unique "absolute good" upon which there seems to be unanimous consensus. The resulting distortions of human experience are difficult to summarize concisely, but might be said to include: compulsive competition; pervasive hyper-specialization; a ubiquitous capitulation to mechanomorphic ideals (both in the realms of thought and those of the body); want of textured appreciation of the diversity and vicissitudes of life itself; and a widespread and barely concealed disdain for weakness, failure, doomed gestures, tragedy, paralysis, fragility, mediocrity, and the ordinary in all its forms (this despite there being excellent evidence that this litany epitomizes much that is essential to human being).

EXPERIENCE

A (the?) category of (uniquely human?) sentience.
Because of the degree to which it affects perception,
experience is the object in one way or another of nearly
all humanistic and social scientific inquiry. Because of the
degree to which it affects perception, experience is that
which is absolutely forbidden to those who undertake
such inquiry.

A
B
C
D
E
F
G
H
I
J
K
L
M
N
O
P
Q
R
S
T
U
V
W
X
Y
Z

EXPERTISE

Training in a particular domain of theory or practice, especially when that training is rare among the general population. Like ERUDITION, expertise is vested in an individual. It entitles him/her to dispense an evaluation, opinion, or judgment over and against the objection of a person who lacks comparable credentials. The expert, as the "knower of," may find his/her inverse in the AMATEUR, or "lover of." It is characteristic of expertise that the expert has repressed his/her affection for a topic in order to acquire, sharpen, and demonstrate a mastery of it. Whether it is formally contradictory or merely unusual for knowledge and love to conciliate (in the sublunary) remains a contested question. Regardless, this basic immiscibility tends to be strongly marked within professions, which do not foster affectionate or enthusiastic display (see PROFESSION). Hence the comedy of a twelve-year-old who self-identifies as an "expert" in international relations—a puerile boast that occasions suspicion and playful indulgence precisely because the manifest enthusiasm is totally incommensurable with the very notion of expertise. The history of the term predicates expertise on the accumulation of EXPERIENCE. But etymology, in this case, may be misleading. While it is true that experts have considerable experience in their respective areas of expertise (i.e., having spent substantial time in careful study), it is by no means clear that experts *acquire* their expertise from said experience. Insofar as it implies the "mastery" of a given technique, expertise arguably *substitutes* for experience in the encounter with an object: it is the capacity to manage—whether that management be taxonomical, historical, manual, etc.— what others find curious or strange.

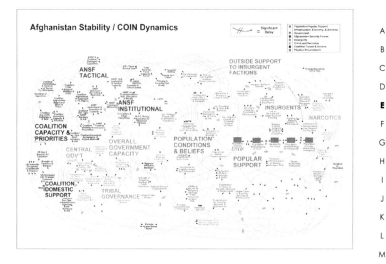

Universities, firms, and states number among the entities
that exist in order to identify, produce, and deploy
expertise, which has been particularly important in law
since the middle of the nineteenth century. The expert
is one who may testify before a court by virtue of his/
her unique ability to elucidate the facts of a case. Such an
arrangement—having an epistemic advantage upon the
accused, the accuser, the jury, and the judge alike—is both
powerful and dubious. The courtroom vests the expert
with the duty to explain the truth "behind" a set of facts;
accordingly, it withdraws the expert from the community
of individuals who are entitled to or forgiven for their
non-knowledge. It is therefore not surprising that the
expert often exhibits symptoms of paranoia characterized
by a disavowal of contingency and a conviction that every
fact may be (indeed, must be) explained according to

(often secret, or concealed) necessity. This predicament may exemplify the tragedy of expertise in general, a regime, as Max Weber suggested, that emerged from the specialization of the educated workforce during the nineteenth and twentieth centuries. It is possible to argue that expertise defines the primary nexus of information and being in modern culture and generates a reflex for the self-surpassing of knowledge in human activity. Perhaps expertise is less the affliction of lone *sçavants* than it is the paranoia of the post-industrial economy itself.

FIELD

The body of topics, concerns, and activities annexed
to a given branch of knowledge; commonly, "field of
study." In general usage, the term "field" is adjacent to
and loosely synonymous or interchangeable with both
SUBJECT and DISCIPLINE. Fields, insofar as they may
refer to both professional and academic enterprise (e.g.,
both to endocrinological and to Renaissance studies),
suspend the arguable separation between professions
and disciplines. Nevertheless, in current parlance,
"field" covers more ground than the scholastically
connotative "subject," whose application in the classroom
hardly extends to the workplace. In the wonderland of
ACADEMIA, a field is a veritable Alice, which is to say, an
entity with variable dimensions when measured against
subjects and disciplines. On the one hand, a scholar may
call his/her field a subset of interests circumscribed by a
broader academic designation. The field-coverage model
endemic to English departments, for instance, refers to
historical periods and, most recently, sociological and
geopolitical categories as "fields" constitutive of literary
studies at large. By contrast, a field may indicate a set of
disciplines collectively (like a post-graduate version of
the elementary "subject"), and thereby communicate less
specificity (or, as it were, offset the punitive overtones
of "discipline"). "Field" itself explicitly activates
spatial connotations absent from either "subject" or
"discipline." Curiously, the literalism of a physical
field reenters the academic context in the aspect of
scientific or, in some cases, social scientific "fieldwork,"
conducted outside the classroom and intended to
develop practical, and sometimes professional, skills.
Perhaps an ostensibly pedestrian synonym for "field"

A
B
C
D
E
F
G
H
I
J
K
L
M
N
O
P
Q
R
S
T
U
V
W
X
Y
Z

such as "territory," however, has latent relevance to the
distribution of intellectual property among disciplines
and departments—or, by a reverse logic, a professional or
academic "occupation" parses to a territorial claim? The
coded assumption of territoriality reinforces speculation
that, in fact, an academic field is a deceptively hospitable
habitat for competitive gazelles engaged in eternal inter-
and intra-generational conflict over circumscribed tracts
of grassland.

FTE

An acronym for "Full-Time Equivalent." A notion
borrowed from government accounting statistics, and
of considerable, rising importance to UNIVERSITY
governance, the FTE represents a unit in the calculation
of labor: one FTE is equal to the full-time work of a
single individual within a given time range (generally a
semester or nine-month "year" in the academic setting).
The size and power of a department or program at a
university is often measured in FTEs, which provide
a metric for comparison across the academic human
resource pool. From an administrative perspective,
FTEs enable the division of faculty members among
different institutional entities. A single individual—for
instance, a philosopher—may be tallied as "half an FTE
in the Philosophy department" and "half an FTE in
the new Center for Human and Non-Human Ethics
and Small Animal Welfare." That latter program may,
under certain circumstances, "loan" its portion of the
philosopher's FTE to the "Program in Irish Studies."
Departmental chairs and deans spend considerable time
apportioning FTEs and managing FTE "budgets" (NB:
in the reductive if clarificatory terms of the Finance
Office, an FTE amounts to a sum of money). While
one might dismiss the FTE as mere administralia, the
birth and death of academic programs is inextricable
from contestation over FTEs. A new program or center
that does not control any FTEs must perpetually solicit
faculty time/labor from other campus entities for
teaching and/or programming. Administrative control
over a body of FTEs can be understood as a valuable
proxy for discipline formation within the modern
university.

A
B
C
D
E
F
G
H
I
J
K
L
M
N
O
P
Q
R
S
T
U
V
W
X
Y
Z

GENRE

The kind, sort, or style of an art-object (see ART). To
classify by genre is to exercise an ancient reflex. In
the *Republic*, Plato divided poetry into the mimetic
and the non-mimetic; in the *Poetics*, Aristotle further
divided mimesis into tragedy and comedy. Subsequent
writers spoke of dithyrambs, satires, and elegies. Indeed,
a kind of atavism inheres in a word that hails from
gens, meaning "kind," "family," or "race." Genre sorts
artifacts according to their commonalities. When one
sees a genre, one imagines lines of filiation and descent,
reversion to an ancestral type or variation from it.
Northrop Frye believed that the West had unlearned
to taxonomize because humanists after the eighteenth
century reacted against that impulse so central to
Linnaeus and his heirs (e.g., Humboldt, Darwin,
Mayr). As naturalists dealt perhaps the decisive blow to
human beings' sense of cosmic isolation and superiority,
Romantics and, later, Modernists insisted upon it: they
taught that artists should express individual will, or, in
default of that, that they should at least "make it new."
There's a hint of the resulting distaste for genre in the
dismissive adjective, "generic." Dime novels, country
songs, and sitcoms are generic; the avant-garde is not.
Some scholars have observed a characteristic reluctance
among artists to admit that art is by and large the
production and reproduction of very similar stuff, and
these scholars have engaged theories of social, cultural,
and psychological structure in order to account for the
family resemblance. But one may not need a theory
of what genre *is* in order to understand what genre
does. After all, genre is that rare construct which one
encounters in the classroom or scholarly journal and

actually applies in the workshop or studio. Apart from an eccentric handful of artists who vociferate upon their absolute departure from precedent (and isn't dissimilarity a form of similarity?), creative individuals tend explicitly to take from those they admire, and tend explicitly to hope to be taken from in turn. Even the strongest poets form coteries and imitate their friends. They write reviews and curate exhibits of work they enjoy. Critics tend to flatter themselves by assigning relative value to this or that object, but they might do well to expiate that neurosis elsewhere. For longer than the historical record can show, artifacts have been made from other artifacts precisely that they may resemble them. Families infuriate and sicken; but they also welcome, shelter, and console.

A
B
C
D
E
F
G
H
I
J
K
L
M
N
O
P
Q
R
S
T
U
V
W
X
Y
Z

GRADUATE STUDENT

Literally (and perhaps paradoxically), a student who
has already "graduated." Which is to say, graduate
students have already completed an undergraduate
degree at a four-year college or university (or the
equivalent), but desire to maintain ties to a pedagogical
milieu. Some do so for the purpose of professional
advancement in defined professional fields (e.g.,
business, law, medicine, architecture). Others seek
supplementary accreditation in the form of potentially
marketable "Master's" degrees in the humanities,
sciences, and social sciences. Still others pursue
an M.F.A. degree, which permits several years of
absorbing dedication to creative production in the
arts (with very little prospect of gainful employment
thereafter). A small number entertain ambitions for
the terminal university degree, known as a doctorate
or Ph.D. Of this last group, those studying the
sciences and engineering tend to work mostly on a
specific laboratory or field project overseen by a senior
researcher in the chosen discipline; such students
are nearly all subsidized by grants secured by these
principal investigators. Students on the Ph.D. track
in the HUMANITIES (who are funded, as a rule, by their
universities directly, out of operating budgets) are
generally abandoned to the alluring (if, also, frequently
harrowing) solitude of reading and writing—at least
for a time. It should be noted, however, that graduate
students offer universities a tempting labor pool, in that
graduate EDUCATION creates a local aggregation of low-
paid educators. Is such TEACHING experience a special
privilege? A valuable apprenticeship in a chosen trade?
Or merely a mode of exploitation? Opinions differ

widely on this matter, an increasingly urgent concern in the wake of academic job market stagnation and identifiably "neoliberal" university reforms.

A
B
C
D
E
F
G
H
I
J
K
L
M
N
O
P
Q
R
S
T
U
V
W
X
Y
Z

HISTORY

A term of some ambiguity, meaning as it does both
the past and the study of the past. This unfortunate
conjunction has occasioned a good deal of confusion,
historically. As a disciplinary formation within the
modern landscape of research and teaching in institutions
of post-secondary learning, history is sometimes
classified with the social sciences and at other times
with the HUMANITIES. This taxonomic ambivalence
reflects multiple genealogies for the enterprise as a
whole, which are themselves reflected in divergences of
practice among professional historians: on the one hand,
a preponderance of such practitioners understand their
primary OBJECTS to be persons (their collective and
individual experiences, conditions, and activities); on
the other hand, a smaller but still significant community
prefer to focus their energies on larger structures or
dynamics (e.g., the state, the economy). The latter tend to
do work that is more easily assimilable to the enterprises
of economists and political scientists; the former tend to
do work that feels more germane to students of literature
and culture. That said, there is, in practice, a fair bit of
overlap (and some back-and-forth) across these domains,
and even those scholars working at the extreme antipodal
verges of this distribution can recognize each other as
historians. The explanation for this has less to do with a
shared theory of historical knowledge as such, or a shared
account of the proper object of historical inquiry, or even
with a shared conception of the proper BIBLIOGRAPHY
for training historians, and more to do, it would seem,
with a pervasive and robustly conserved notion of *what
historical labor looks like* (see INTELLECTUAL LABOR).
Which is to say, historians recognize what counts as the

work of a historian. Essential to this shared formation: the archive. Broadly speaking, and with almost no exceptions, historians, to be historians, must spend some time recovering stuff about the past from collations of documentary source material that hails from the past-period in question. The exceptions here (e.g., classical historians) tend to prove the rule, in that such marginal cases (historians of the classical period tend not to have access to archives, and must work from established texts) tend to be found with much reduced frequency within history departments themselves (a classical historian will be more likely found in a department of classics). The same dynamic can be identified among "ethnohistorians" and those historically concerned with non-literate peoples: neither group is well represented in actual departments of history. When it comes to distribution requirements for undergraduates, a number of colleges and universities require some exposure to "Historical Analysis" or the equivalent. Interestingly, the determination of which undergraduate courses ought to be designated as fulfilling such requirements can become a bone of contention for scholars with appointments in history departments, in that university deans and administrators (not to mention students and parents) frequently believe that many courses in many departments review a great deal of material from the past, and therefore merit to be designated as bearing history-credit for bureaucratic purposes. Professional historians will often dissent from this view, and a close, participatory ethnography of their community discussions on this apparently marginal matter would offer rich (if oblique) insight into just what historians think history actually is

A
B
C
D
E
F
G
H
I
J
K
L
M
N
O
P
Q
R
S
T
U
V
W
X
Y
Z

at any given time. Such an analysis is beyond the scope of this keyword definition, but it is notable (if confusing, given what has been said above) that work with archival sources is seldom, in fact, a component of undergraduate courses in history. Be that as it may, there is a broader fact about disciplinary history that merits particular attention in the context of reflections on inter-, trans-, and anti-disciplinarity; to wit, historians tend not only to adhere to (and practice) an extremely exacting and austere form of *historicism* (meaning here, that orientation to the stuff of the world that privileges the temporal address—or "place in time"—of a given person, idea, phenomenon, artifact, etc. over all other features), but also to act, within learned settings, as something like the arbiters or even the *police-enforcers* of historicism. In much the same way that philosophers might be accused of perpetually endeavoring to extend their commitment to ubiquitous non-contradiction *into* and even *under* adjacent university activities (despite conceptual contradiction being effectively constitutive of human endeavor as such), historians can be thought of as sensing themselves in possession of a comparably ineluctable and primary intellectual enterprise: putting things where they belong in time. And this despite there being a good deal of philosophical evidence that time itself does not even exist (as well as the broad anecdotal evidence that human beings live only in the present). It is not merely that historians tend to consider violations of historicist thinking "wrong"; it is also that they tend to consider considerations of things other than historicist thinking substantially *misguided*. Interdisciplinary encounters with historians therefore often involve the historian pointing out that what the non-historical colleague is doing should be historicized (see CROSS-DISCIPLINARY STERILITY). In this way, disciplinary history seems particularly subject to "mission creep" when permitted cosmopolitan peregrinations within a university setting. In view of what can be descried as the fundamental limitations of historicism as an activity of mind, this kudzu-like characteristic of professional historical thought merits close scrutiny.

A
B
C
D
E
F
G
H
I
J
K
L
M
N
O
P
Q
R
S
T
U
V
W
X
Y
Z

HUMANITIES

The plural of "humanity," used to refer to the totality
of mammalian creatures gathered under the taxonomic
binomial *Homo sapiens*. In mood, the term invokes the
human collective across time and space, though the word
tends to emerge in aspirational contexts, frequently
inflected by ethical concern (both genuine and feigned).
It might be said that *Homo sapiens* designates not only
"human beings" but also the promise of an objective
or impartial designation of membership in the human
community; whereas "humanity" designates the same
collective while implicitly denying the validity or
adequacy of any non-normative designation of that
community. Interestingly, the plural term, "humanities,"
has come to have a very distinct meaning at some remove
from the semantic field of the singular form. In practice,
the specific locution "the humanities" (always with the
definite article; "humanistic" in the adjectival form)
refers to a set of academic disciplines: canonically those
involving the study (though not, actually, the making)
of works of art, literature, and music, together with the
enterprise of historical inquiry and certain traditions of
philosophy. It is difficult to account for the conceptual
coherence of these domains, taken as a whole, and it is
further difficult to distinguish them from the sciences
(which are themselves diverse; see SCIENCE). Such
parsing has become more difficult as all of the disciplinary
formations of the modern university have gradually
accommodated themselves to a fundamentally scientific
structure (meaning that all are committed to progressive
KNOWLEDGE PRODUCTION under conditions of
PEER REVIEW by researchers with specialized EXPERTISE
in given domains, generally figured as "disciplines"; see

DISCIPLINE). Nevertheless, the distinction between the humanities and the sciences has been a prominent feature of colleges and universities for at least a century, and the roots reach back quite deep in the intellectual traditions of the modern world (to such an extent that commentary on these matters is, and has been for some time, itself a significant academic enterprise—though in the humanities only; scientists seem, as a rule, without concern for the problem). It is sometimes pointed out that the older dichotomy in university life—the primary division that preceded the rise of the natural and physical sciences as university activities—was the humanities and the divinities (see THEOLOGY), and that it is only with the substantial disappearance of the latter category of learning that the humanities found themselves juxtaposed with the sciences. The rise of the social sciences out of the late-Enlightenment work of Saint-Simon and Comte has further vexed the question of what the humanities actually are and do, since substantial portions of what might have been understood as their purview (history, for instance; what comes to be thought of as anthropology; also much of the formal study of language and behavior) have come to be powerfully engaged by enterprises that eschew the language, modes, and general tenor of *Humanismus*. In practice, the study of human beings and their many artifacts, traditions, productions, and preoccupations has been, over the last two centuries, increasingly handled by individuals with little use for the term "humanities," and relatively little connection to the hermeneutic traditions and classical master-texts that create the general climate of humanistic endeavor in its university form. It can be argued persuasively that

A
B
C
D
E
F
G
H
I
J
K
L
M
N
O
P
Q
R
S
T
U
V
W
X
Y
Z

the humanities amount to a thinly-veiled metaphysical enterprise (of dubious pith and integrity), resulting from a secular dilapidation of the theological programs that once gave both primary and final meaning to the category of the human (see METAPHYSICS). Strident anti-humanisms of various species (Foucauldian, Deleuzian, Kittlerian) can be understood to be decrying exactly this woozily delusional aspect of the humanities, and the virulence of some of these attacks can perhaps be seen to reflect impatience with an air of complacency (or even wounded dignity) projected by some partisans of the humanistic tradition. At the same time, it is easy to be anxious about the long-term social and political effects of abandoning any and all efforts to spangle the category *Homo sapiens* with metaphysical sequins of some sort. This granted, one may well ask: Who is to be trusted with such work? Out of what shall the flash be fashioned? One is, at present, without good answers to these significant questions. But it may be that the humanities are (or will be?) relevant in this regard.

INTELLECTUAL LABOR

A form of labor regularly distinguished from manual labor.
Intellectual labor is characterized as more closely related
to, or dependent on, the workings of the mind or brain.
Increasingly, such thought-work has been categorized as
the enterprise conducted by a certain class of individuals
(i.e., intellectuals) and a certain class of occupations (e.g.,
university professors). As such, intellectual labor not only
has become a term used to explain a form of labor, but
also has been established as a type of professional behavior
expected, demanded, and crudely measured. These
classifications and professional developments reveal several
lines of tension and present meaningful problems, to wit:
whether it is plausible to draw lines between intellectual
labor and manual labor (and/or between intellectual labor
and non-intellectual labor); whether (regardless of how
carefully such line-drawing might be done) it will always
be the case that there are many kinds of manual labor that,
performed in a specific way or approached by the right
individual, could take on a profoundly cerebral quality;
whether any effort to distinguish between those who use
their brain for labor and those who don't (or those who
don't "as much," or "as well") can ever be anything other
than an arrogant and/or condescending exercise in class
prejudice, etc. Perhaps the question is more scientific than
it initially appears (though this is obviously the move to
intellectualize *par excellence*), and all one need do is insert
within each laborer a sophisticated monitor capable of
establishing how (and where) the brain is functioning
activity-to-activity, task-to-task. In addition to the stated
difficulty of classifying the boundaries of intellectual
labor, problems abound in occupations that have come
to be defined by their commitment to this form of work.

A
B
C
D
E
F
G
H
I
J
K
L
M
N
O
P
Q
R
S
T
U
V
W
X
Y
Z

Take, as a relevant example, ACADEMIA and professional academics. To the extent that intellectual labor is understood as a (the?) primary duty of modern academics, questions arise as to the preferred kinds of intellectual labor and the manner in which such labor can be evaluated. Different departments and universities have come to prioritize some species of intellectual labor over others, although it is not always clear that these prioritizations are publically justified (or even conscious). Relatedly, the value and effect of intellectual labor are not easy to assess. Several criteria may be invoked, including: the number of hours spent laboring ("I saw you clocked in a few minutes late yesterday, Steve!"); the quality of publications ("Damn, that was a persuasive article, Steve!"); the selectivity of the journal that accepts said publications ("Ooh, isn't that venue a tad bush-league, Steve?") (see EXCELLENCE). All of the above may be ways of tracking the intellectual impact of an academic's work on the academic community or broader public (see AUDIENCE), or they may be secondary to a more holistic mode of evaluation ("Have you heard of Steve?"). One final point on the nature and space of intellectual work: those occupations that consider themselves predicated on intellectual labor may incur grave losses when an obsession concerning its supply and demand displaces and depreciates other essential virtues, practices, or activities. When the life and the effective exercise of the mind become detached from other human goods (when, say, incrementally surpassing previous learning in a highly specialized subdisciplinary subregion becomes the *summum bonum* of academic life) intellectual labor may neglect its greatest and most rewarding tasks. (Or are they even tasks?)

INTERDISCIPLINARITY

Literally, that which lies "between" the disciplines.
Hence, in principle, a domain not policed by them. In
practice, such spaces have lately been used as marginal
zones wherein labor propaedeutic to discipline
formation may occur. However, in the context of
mounting institutional and/or economic pressure on
the humanities, such spaces may increasingly serve in
the manner of refugee camps for scholars, teachers, and
students no longer sheltered by disciplinary structures, or
seeking escape from same.

A
B
C
D
E
F
G
H
I
J
K
L
M
N
O
P
Q
R
S
T
U
V
W
X
Y
Z

INTERPRETATION

The activity of seeking and/or conveying meaning, especially the meaning of an object understood to carry, reveal, or secrete something worth attending to. Interpretation requires the hypothesis that meaning lies above, below, behind, or within the object (the choice of metaphor will be a consistent and revealing theme), by virtue of which the attention lavished upon it may be justified, or at least explained. As a heuristic, one may adopt the distinction between interpretation and description, the latter of which purports not to convey the meaning of an object but rather to reproduce its features. In the HUMANITIES, descriptive work tends to concentrate on form (e.g., lyric, film), technique (e.g., meter, montage), and style (e.g., Sapphic, Neorealist) — in sum, what one might call "effects." Interpretation, by contrast, tends toward social, political, and psychological "causes." The binary has considerably less purchase within the modern sciences, though why this should be the case remains opaque, particularly when one considers that the distinction was well marked in the *history* of science (e.g., natural history vs. natural philosophy). Polemicists in the academy have made interpretation into a wedge between arbitrary and disreputable factions: on one hand, proponents of "depth interpretation," who define their project as the discovery of latent meaning; on the other hand, proponents of "surface interpretation," who dismiss latent meaning as a neurotic projection of the interpreter him/herself, and define their own project as a return to meaning that is manifest. To the sociologist, the issue may be the narcissism of minor difference: the parties, it could be argued, commonly exaggerate their "ideological" conflicts precisely in order to conceal the remarkable similarity of their labor (writing commentary on canonical texts with a vocabulary casually borrowed from French and German philosophers). One must acknowledge that both schools of interpretation trade on a shared metaphor, namely, that the text and its meaning form a three-dimensional object that exists in Euclidean space; and furthermore, that scholarly work has to do with the proper positioning of oneself at one (or more?) points relative to that object, and hence standing "in relation to" the text-interpretation manifold. All of this betrays the extraordinary difficulty of understanding interpretation in a way that does not presume what interpretation is. Attempts to do so inevitably embarrass the people involved. What is worse, such efforts distract from the urgent task of defending interpretation itself. A hasty review would disclose the enormous variety of interpretive techniques that have influenced western culture—e.g., philology, hermeneutics (Talmudic, Biblical, philosophical, objective, etc.), Marxism, psychoanalysis—and also the ease with which any of them may be said to anticipate (and therefore belong to?) the schools of interpretation that are momentarily fashionable. But none of this can explain why one might interpret an object today. As efforts to outsource interpretation (to machines, to "crowd sourcing") continue, the debate about various *kinds* of interpretation may eventually appear a quaint reminder of a time when interpretation mattered at all.

A
B
C
D
E
F
G
H
I
J
K
L
M
N
O
P
Q
R
S
T
U
V
W
X
Y
Z

IRONY

Notionally, the simultaneity of two (or more) perspectives. Any account of irony must begin with a caveat: if irony were to be successfully defined, it would cease to be useful. The difficulty of clarifying its operations in ordinary language precisely defines the domain within which it can operate. Still, it is not wrong to say that irony *involves a doubleness*; and such a description, as vague as it may be, can nonetheless suggest why irony might be so important for interdisciplinary studies. The greatest risk to interdisciplinarity as an intellectual project is the collapse of its perspectivalism into a monologic METHOD. Interdisciplinarity, that is, depends upon the persistence and the discretion of its constitutive disciplines. The best interdisciplinary thinking arises not from a fusion but from a friction of methods. The interdisciplinarian, therefore, does well to be an ironist, agile among the disciplines, capable of seeing each under the aspect of the others, committed wholesale to none of them. Which is to say that interdisciplinary thinking is not more knowing than the knowledge given by the disciplines on which it depends (as it often claims to be), but less, and that is its value.

KNOWLEDGE PRODUCTION

The means to and/or end of academic life (see IRONY).

A
B
C
D
E
F
G
H
I
J
K
L
M
N
O
P
Q
R
S
T
U
V
W
X
Y
Z

MEDIUM

An object, material, or substance that transfers
information, especially for the benefit of human
individuals. In his annexation of the vast territory
of Foucauldian discourse analysis, Friedrich Kittler
famously asserted that "media determine our situation."
The very technologies, instruments, channels, and devices
that allow for the recording and subsequent accession of
information (and therefore culture) constitute a "technical
a priori," a media *dispositif* that simultaneously structures
people and the messages they study or produce. This was a
techno-deterministic echo of Nietzsche's famous dictum:
our writing tools are also working on our thoughts. With
the proliferation of cognitive and mnemonic prosthetics
in the early twenty-first century, the problem of defining
the object of humanistic (or, for that matter, technical)
inquiry has become increasingly indistinguishable
from this medial question. The tools that allow for
the mechanical processing of information—and that
subsequently produce new transfers and socializations
of knowledge (while transforming the human's attention
span)—are "medium" in that they produce the conditions
for the synthesis of thought across fields, communities,
and various kinds of "records." As *supplementary* to
information, extending and amputating human capacities,
the medium is not a neutral entity. In seventeenth-
century and early eighteenth-century science, the singular
"medium" referred to an intermediate agent or substance
that allowed phenomena to appear (as in ether). The
term acquired increasingly technical connotations across
the long nineteenth century, leading to its application
to specialized modes of communication (as in print).
Divergent understandings of the term were in the

second half of the twentieth century synthesized in the
theorization of the plural "media," a term that designates
the multiple conditions of transmission that constitute the
relationship between a material form and a sign system.
This terminological pluralization serves not to flatten the
differentiated aesthetics of particular media, but rather
to highlight the multiplicity of registers—sometimes not
aesthetic but, for instance, socio-political—that contribute
to the production and reception of meaning systems.
While historical understandings of technical media
(photography, the novel, cinema, etc.) have become part
of distinct disciplines (history of photography, literary
studies, film studies), more recent theories of media
emphasize the processual ontologies of communication
structures, and in doing so create analyses that cut
across the established disciplinary boundaries. This shift
toward the analysis of operations has developed into new
methodological and institutional configurations such as
Kulturtechniken and comparative media, which seek to
investigate practices of inscription across assorted fields,
such as acoustic engineering, psychoanalysis, disability
studies, and many others. The novelty of such formations
notwithstanding, it should be noted that the study of
technical media such as film has always provided sites for
interdisciplinary inquiry and reflection. Colloquial uses of
"medium" support this transdisciplinary understanding.
The reconciliatory expression "happy medium" and the
moderating "medium-rare" suggest on the one hand the
defiance of an idealized state (as in a dogmatic purity, or
the state of being fully cooked) and on the other mark a
qualitative, and therefore interestingly imprecise, state of
indeterminacy.

A
B
C
D
E
F
G
H
I
J
K
L
M
N
O
P
Q
R
S
T
U
V
W
X
Y
Z

METAPHYSICS

The questions without answers to which inquiry cannot begin, or perhaps conclude. In terms of difficulty, it is advanced; in terms of order, fundamental. To illustrate: "What is *metaphysics*?"; better, "What *is* metaphysics?"; better still, "*What* is metaphysics?"

METHOD

A technology for the production of consensus. Methods
exist as sources of confidence in objects of knowledge or
study (see OBJECT). They claim predictable outcomes
as well as the logical correspondence between these
outcomes and the practices that produced them. This
sociological aspect of method was suggested in the
1930s by the Polish-Jewish physician and microbiologist
Ludwick Fleck, who wrote about "communities of
thought" woven through consensual engagement in
observational practices. While method in some cases
seeks a prevailing objectivity, Fleck's community of
thought articulated an understanding of method that
left room for the acceptance of provisional truths. In this
way, methods can be understood to have legacies: they
are transmitted, abandoned, and sometimes revived.
One especially famous and highly narcissistic method,
however, waged a prominent and influential crusade
against doubt, and did so by positing an epistemology
ostensibly indifferent to all historical, pragmatic, and/
or communal foundations for truth (and access to it).
Descartes's method (i.e., The Method), in its radical
disavowal of tradition and emphasis on the solitary,
internal quest for access to the absolute, yielded a version
of modernity founded on reason as a model for human
progress. The Cartesian method of systematization
eventually infiltrated humanistic modes of thought.
Thus methodologies, often explained in introductions
to written texts, purport to ensure access to knowledge
on the basis of their freedom from bias or inconsistency
(see METHODOLOGY). Whatever the status of truth
as a methodological target, each method represents a
disciplinary tool. Like the letter-size format, which fits

A
B
C
D
E
F
G
H
I
J
K
L
M
N
O
P
Q
R
S
T
U
V
W
X
Y
Z

any individual's sheet of paper into any other's binder,
a method implies transferability and facilitates sharing.
However, the application of a standard American
three-hole punch to an A4 document produces notable
disconformities.

METHODOLOGY

Especially in research-oriented disciplines, the system
or logic of methods in the aggregate (see METHOD).
By one account, the relationship between method and
methodology resembles that between the part and the
whole, where a method, or a set thereof, occupies a larger
research framework. The distinction between the specific
and the general provides another analogous model,
where some method(s) instantiate(s) a wider research
ethos or program. Still further, and in the sense suggested
by its etymology, methodology relates to method as
theory relates to practice. "Methodology" combines
"method" with "-ology," which designates the study of
some field or object, and thus implies the analysis of
analytical strategies themselves. In this way, methodology
asks questions of methods in order to articulate their
operative logic. The full ramifications of methodological
thought reflect the manifold potentialities of theory
itself. Methodology might seek to demonstrate the
integrity, accuracy, relevance, reproducibility, and/or
efficacy of methods, for instance, much as theory can
be said to substantiate, explicate, defend, codify, and/
or regulate practices. In effect, layering, as it does, over
method, methodology builds accountability and self-
critique into research scholarship. However, in "softer"
humanistic disciplines largely bereft of (or indifferent
to) quantifiable data, a rhetoric of interpretive practices
displaces one of research methods. That said, "theory" in
this domain has, since the theoretical turn of the 1970s,
come to designate a consolidated critical enterprise
with some transdisciplinary purchase. Insofar as theory
operates alongside methodology, the humanities call
for a more nuanced distinction between the two terms.

A
B
C
D
E
F
G
H
I
J
K
L
M
N
O
P
Q
R
S
T
U
V
W
X
Y
Z

Namely, if theory supplies an analytical framework for interpretation, which overtakes research in certain humanistic fields, what is the methodological remainder? The concurrence of theory with methodology jeopardizes the relay between either term and the scholarly activities it ostensibly describes. To the extent that methodology is incompatible with theory, it transforms a scholarly program into a tactical agenda that determines— rather than derives from—interpretive practices. Ironically, methodology here risks the suspension of the self-conscious attitude it otherwise affords (see OCCUPATIONAL HAZARD).

MODEL

A representation of a thing, or, what is very different, the ideal of that thing. In other words, a model is generated and generative. Since a model is never the thing itself, one is presented with a loss of fidelity to the real thing through varied degrees of abstraction or partial sight. Witness, below, a photograph of penguins at the London Zoo examining a model of their future home (designed by the architecture firm Tecton in 1934) and an illustrated map of Sir Thomas More's Utopia.

Models rely on analogy or metaphor; this technique advances specific modes of viewing and thinking about the modeled subject and may bring new levels of clarity to areas of interest, often through the obfuscation of other modes or foci of viewing. The constellation of academic disciplines can be schematized in a number of ways ("constellation," itself a model, evokes a way of imagining this environment): as an ecosystem or a confederation of nation-states, as a branching tree, a lineage, a network of nodes, and so on. Each model raises new questions: whether certain disciplines are

A
B
C
D
E
F
G
H
I
J
K
L
M
N
O
P
Q
R
S
T
U
V
W
X
Y
Z

borne out of others; whether some disciplines share
symbiotic relations, while others, antagonistic; whether
disciplines are amenable to interaction and exchange
and, if they are, in what terms (see DISCIPLINE). Models
presuppose superlatives—some best object, method, or
product of research—and insist that scholars, students,
and researchers target paragons, even on those (quite
frequent) occasions when an ostensible "best" is
hopelessly caught between verisimilitude and ideality
(see EXCELLENCE). Models should therefore be handled
with caution.

NEW CRITICISM

A style of INTERPRETATION made popular and
arguably obsolete in English departments during the
twentieth century. If John Crowe Ransom baptized
"New Criticism" with his 1941 essay of that name, I. A.
Richards wrote its sacred scripture. *Practical Criticism*
debuted in 1929, and saw several printings and three
editions in the following decade. Part textbook, part
scratchwork, part manifesto, the book held a canonical
status in the syllabi at Cambridge, where William
Empson was Richards's student, and at several colleges
in the United States. At a time when the HUMANITIES
vied for legitimacy with expanding programs in the
natural and social sciences, New Criticism provided a
strategy for literary studies: poems, like problems, could
be solved. New Criticism relied on a method stunning for
its simplicity—what has come to be called "close reading."
Isolating the poem from its context, students learned to
identify patterns within the work itself. There was an
interest in form (e.g., that rhyme may indicate a hitherto
unseen relationship between words, or that the sound of a
line may run against its sense), but not only. New Critics
wagered that the poem, understood as a whole, bore
all of the information necessary for its interpretation.
Empson spoke of the poet's (and sometimes the
poem's) "unconscious"; W. K. Wimsatt of its "unity"
and "organization"; Cleanth Brooks of its "essential
structure." If close reading could slip now and again into
a vicious circle (all clues for interpretation are contained
in the poem itself, by virtue of its being poetry, and yet
good poems are distinct from bad poems on the grounds
that some contain better clues than others), the method
nevertheless met a pressing need. Poetry wanted to look

A
B
C
D
E
F
G
H
I
J
K
L
M
N
O
P
Q
R
S
T
U
V
W
X
Y
Z

like SCIENCE, and New Criticism made for it a bespoke disguise. Throughout *Practical Criticism* and later works like *Poetry and Science*, Richards went out of his way to handle poems as if they were natural artifacts susceptible to experiment and control. As against "preconceptions" and "stock-responses," he preached reading "with a view toward advancing our knowledge of what may be called the natural history of human opinions and feelings." The idea determined the book from the top down: poems were presented without attribution, and read without help from HISTORY. For the "advancement of poetry," it was essential to cultivate objective judgment. Although New Criticism fancied itself a humanist approximation of the sciences, it is not obvious that literary interpretation could accede to that logic whereby hypotheses are entertained and dismissed. The propositions in *Practical Criticism* were numbered conspicuously like those in the *Tractatus Logico-Philosophicus*, and given that Wittgenstein's text would have been much discussed at Cambridge, Richards may have had the MODEL in mind. But if Richards, like Wittgenstein, imagined his book a ladder, it is difficult in the end to envision him asking his readers to kick it aside after they had finished with it. The New Critics believed their conclusions were not just true, but good. That they could not be falsified. The stoicism so moving at the end of Wittgenstein's precocious masterpiece, the utter refusal of its own authority, is a scientism for which literary study yet longs. One might ask what would happen should it be granted its wish. Automation of its practices, perhaps?

OBJECT

A text, material, or concept of scholarly investigation; commonly, "object of study." (Also, often, a "medium-sized dry good.") Objects predicate methods and range widely within humanistic inquiry, from forms of concrete evidence (e.g., written documents, material artifacts) to conceptual structures (e.g., traditions of thought, systems of belief), to phenomenal agents (e.g., social forces, cultural patterns), and so on (see METHOD). Where humanistic research engages a human population, the object toggles across the subject/object divide. Likewise, by a metonymic operation, a scholar's object of study may refer to that subject which identifies his/her entire discipline or field. Where "subject" designates a given topic or theme under discussion, it represents an object of local attention. Virtually inexhaustible and rhetorically slippery, objects also resist conclusive classification by discipline, as well as stable identification according to precedent, genre, or type. Objects migrate between disciplines as a function of interdisciplinary study or institutional change, and often simply occupy wider disciplinary space (see INTERDISCIPLINARITY). It is possible that an identifiable drift in the direction of the interdisciplinary study of "objects" (in the "medium-sized dry good" sense) indexes a general pandering to the commodity fetishisms of a dominant consumer culture— aided, perhaps, by broadly reduced patience with the specific eye- and mind-labor of reading a TEXT.

A
B
C
D
E
F
G
H
I
J
K
L
M
N
O
P
Q
R
S
T
U
V
W
X
Y
Z

OCCUPATIONAL HAZARD

An incentive for caution in work-related circumstances. (*Academic*) The risk of insufficient or excessive self-awareness.

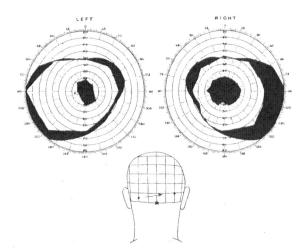

PEER REVIEW

A significant "social technology" in the modern
university system. Peer review has become the ubiquitous
mechanism whereby research is evaluated within
academic life. In practice, peer review may take many
forms, but the essential core of the enterprise involves
the sending of an instance of scholarly labor (an article
draft or published book, a fellowship proposal or
tenure dossier, etc.) to one or, better, an array (panel,
COMMITTEE, etc.) of peers (other academics understood
to be actively engaged in or near the subject of the work
in question) who (often, but not always, anonymously)
assess the merits and demerits of the material. These
evaluations tend to take the form of written comments
and/or criticism, but administrative shorthands (in the
form of numerical grades or letters) are sometimes used.
The sum of such "peer reviews" is taken to be a reliable
index of the merits of the work (though the "summation"
of diverse narrative analyses often proves challenging,
not to say arbitrary), and publication decisions, together
with significant allocations of institutional resources
(e.g., salary, honors), are now wholly contingent on
the outcome of peer review processes. While mutual
evaluation—explicit and implicit, direct and indirect,
anonymous and personal—has been a feature of social
life across most cultures and most historical periods, the
fetishization of peer review as a distinctive instrument
of KNOWLEDGE PRODUCTION within universities is
not easy to understand. The (pseudo-?) formalization of
such procedures would seem to participate in the general
movement of modern societies toward more elaborately
bureaucratic social forms. In addition, the distribution
of such decision-making and its systematic embedment

A
B
C
D
E
F
G
H
I
J
K
L
M
N
O
P
Q
R
S
T
U
V
W
X
Y
Z

within communities of inquiry can be understood
to reflect a specifically administrative or regulatory
activation of an older notion of a "republic of letters." To
reprise an analytic quip often applied to democracy, peer
review may be the worst system conceivable for doing
the work it must do—except for all the others. Though it
should be said that a number of significant non-university
domains do not use peer review, and seem to function
nevertheless. Neither governments nor commercial
enterprises have engaged the method in any important
way. Closer, perhaps, to university life, trade publishers
of books and journalism also forego the form, though
their basic activities—receiving and evaluating texts for
publication—are substantially conformal with the work
of university presses and scholarly journals. Works of
merit (and works of little merit) surface in peer-review
and non-peer-review venues alike. However, works of
disciplinary merit appear almost exclusively in the former,
since non-peer-review work largely fails to clear a primary
test of disciplinary knowledge formation: explicit
engagement with (or is it thralldom to?) the disciplinary
"conversation." It is worth noting that the sum total of
all peer reviews written in a given field is perhaps a more
faithful representation of that disciplinary conversation
than the published material that eventuates from this
matrix of mutual commentary and evaluation. Be that
as it may, it is important to observe the extremely recent
emergence of the explicit language of "peer review." *A
keyword search raises almost no relevant instances of the
phrase before 1970*. Moreover, the historical nexus out
of which modern peer review arises is worthy of note:
the earliest usages are closely connected to regulatory

interventions into human experimentation in the Cold War social sciences. The first formal "peer review" panels are effectively the institutional forerunners of modern Institutional Review Boards (IRBs). One may well wonder whether peer review in its currently pervasive form retains any vestige of its origins in anxious efforts by colleges and universities to police sadistic psychologists and thereby limit institutional liability for their practices.

A
B
C
D
E
F
G
H
I
J
K
L
M
N
O
P
Q
R
S
T
U
V
W
X
Y
Z

PRACTICE

Arguably, the application of thoughts; hence, an antonym of "theory," which is the thinking of them. The hackneyed saying that what's good in theory may not be so in practice presents the two as antipodal (if perhaps reciprocal) modes. One finds variants of this implied splitting throughout the descriptive language of academic work that falls between the theoretical and the practical— namely, "applied science" (implying a non-applied science) and "practical arts" (suggesting, suggestively, a series of impractical arts). Practice assumes tangible labor and tangible outcomes, which take the form of technological advances and/or physical products that bear some commercial value. A "practicum," in an academic setting, often refers to seminars or lab courses that emulate situations and environments outside the academy. In common usage, practice (e.g., "to practice medicine," "to practice law," "to have a private practice") is something that professionals do once they are deemed professional by their accrediting body. A scholar will rarely say that he/she "practices" the study of Quattrocento *literatura*, but artists very consistently refer to their "artistic practices." It is possible that this latter usage may reflect the arts taking on the semblance and language of a "scientific" (i.e., progressive, continually self-surpassing, knowledge-producing) activity so as to better fit within the modern university's general orientation. Practice is also used to refer to repetitive training in a field, as one may do on an actual field (e.g., "I am going to baseball practice") or in a disciplinary field (e.g., years of learning and paper-writing prior to a dissertation). In this usage, the term "practice" may apply to all activity prior to one's full acceptance (or professionalization) in a field, along the lines of the familiar adage, "practice makes perfect."

PROFESSION

An occupation that requires specific training, proven
knowledge, and specialized abilities (e.g., medical
doctor, lawyer). The professions have established highly
independent communities, are generally afforded secure
social status, and rely on state power to regulate diverse
occupational dynamics through licensing and other
work guidelines. They can arguably be contrasted in
important ways with disciplines (see DISCIPLINE),
which also generate occupational positions and discrete,
self-regulated communities, but reveal closer ties to
the university than to the state. Certain aspects of the
modern university, however, complicate any clean
contrast between the disciplines and the professions.
For instance, as students, parents, departments, and
university officials seek "financial justification for this
$200,000 investment in Jane," Jane herself may begin to
sense pre-professional pressure. Discussions concerning
job placement, starting salaries, and "practical skills"
imparted through academic effort will be difficult to
avoid. When half the students enrolled in GER 345
("German Idealism in the Nineteenth Century") seek
to join corporate law offices, banking institutions, or
hospitals within a decade of graduating, how does one
meaningfully distinguish the so-called *disciplinary*
project of *Germanistik* from the professional/client
relationships that characterize the professions? Does the
former undergo a mystical transmutation into the latter
when nineteen-year-old Jane (and/or her professor)
isn't looking? Must the German Department attract
in perpetuity a certain number of Janes in order to
perpetuate itself? And if indeed Jane gets a strong letter
of recommendation to law school from the instructor

A
B
C
D
E
F
G
H
I
J
K
L
M
N
O
P
Q
R
S
T
U
V
W
X
Y
Z

of GER 345, is it possible that Jane's ability to perform to the (alien, arbitrary, and possibly tedious) standards of advanced disciplinary German Studies has effectively served as nothing more or less than an index (or proxy?) for her capacities complacently to serve a constructive role in the endless document review that characterizes the discovery phase of complex corporate litigation? The neoliberal university presents numerous conundrums of this sort.

PROGRESS

The gymnastics of moving forward, understood as
advancement or improvement, although possible without
any propulsive motion, as in the case of stationary bikes.

A
B
C
D
E
F
G
H
I
J
K
L
M
N
O
P
Q
R
S
T
U
V
W
X
Y
Z

READING

The activity of assimilating written material, often as indistinct from the activity of INTERPRETATION. The latter sense of the term occurs widely enough that behaviors, situations, or circumstances might likewise be "read." A general penchant for conflating reading and interpretation may well reflect a collective preference for putting carts before horses, or even a reflexive tendency on the part of advanced thinkers to insist that adjacent carts and horses are simply single entities. It should be noted, however, that if a cart-horse complex is moving in reverse (say, rolling downhill), it may in fact be preferable (for the horse) to be in the "rear" (defined by the vector of motion). Which is to say that the cart should in fact always go "before" the horse, backwards (see PROGRESS).

REGULATION

A set of practices and techniques intended to limit variability and individuality; a prioritization of rules, limits, and conventions (rather than exceptions) in the service of reason. Surpassing mere METHOD, formal regulation seeks to produce highly *intentional* objects of knowledge. The modern sense of regulation is derived from the guiding principles that structured religious life, and yet the term has acquired scientific connotations pertaining to measured order as imposed by the French *mètre* (and its *règle*) and by empirical assumptions about natural occurrences (like the so-called "regular" heartbeat). In scholarly environments, the conscious and unconscious governance of disciplines by rules and restrictions—understood as efforts at maintenance— inevitably leads to various strategies of conservativism that subsequently require intellectual "deregulation."

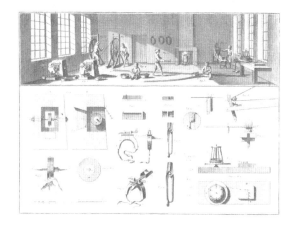

A
B
C
D
E
F
G
H
I
J
K
L
M
N
O
P
Q
R
S
T
U
V
W
X
Y
Z

RIGOR

Austerity, scrupulousness, or inflexibility. But the term
has had a variable career. In the medieval scientific
community, "rigor" meant bodily stiffness and referred
to a physiological effect of illness. Apart from the limit
case, *rigor mortis*, the term could indicate something
internal (a patient's feelings) as well as something *external*
(a patient's symptoms). Thus rigor has always been an
objective ideal with a subjective basis, appearing within
a structure of recognition. A monk might call himself
"rigorous" because of his abstemious rituals, while his
peers might identify him as such by his tonsure and
cassock. It is this general sense of rigor as the performance
or manifestation of rule-bound behavior that has made
the term so useful to disciplines beyond medicine (see
REGULATION). Within the contemporary academy,
rigor is emblematic of the desire to decompose fields
of inquiry into their barest elements. The paradigm for
this is the near-constant effort since the seventeenth
century to establish a secure foundation for mathematics
(see KNOWLEDGE PRODUCTION). Calculus
survived many attempts to axiomatize its technical
procedures, each iteration of the endeavor considered
more irreducibly logical than the last. What is curious
about this example—what is curious about rigor as an
academic concept—is that in aspiration it represents the
a priori foundation for inquiry as such; but in practice it
emerges as an *a posteriori* justification within a partially
consolidated field, as if to stipulate why it is okay to be
doing what is already being done. One might call this
phenomenon "rigorization"—the sociology according to
which what is ingenious, expedient, or simply popular
is made consistent with some (possibly arbitrary)

truth-practice. Humanists have been no less attracted to this idea than mathematicians, and today, rigor is *de rigueur*. A glance at the *New York Times* will confirm its indiscriminate application to food, architecture, and fashion, such that, for instance, one might read of an angular overcoat as a "rigorous interpretation" of its class of outerwear. Rigor has so completely saturated academic discourse that it has become a general term of approbation, something synonymous with the sophistication of text-based argument (see EXCELLENCE). It is therefore tempting to prognosticate that it will soon become *passé*, replaced like so many coats out of season.

A
B
C
D
E
F
G
H
I
J
K
L
M
N
O
P
Q
R
S
T
U
V
W
X
Y
Z

SCHOOL

An institution that functions predominately as a place for
EDUCATION. At the *eschaton*, St. Augustine believed that
the damned would suffer a pain infinitely worse (but no
less embodied) than the pain they felt throughout their
nasty, brutish, and short lives on earth. To vindicate this
unorthodox opinion (it was not clear in fifth-century
THEOLOGY that the body could endure such torment),
the Bishop of Hippo developed a convincing retort:
all have felt inklings of what awaits them at the gates
of Hell from their time in school. Writing *De Civitate
Dei* after his conversion to Christianity, St. Augustine
was inclined to remember his secular education with
acute disdain. But the history of literature is nothing if
not a history of delinquents. Writers like Milton and
Wordsworth have also been moved to despair about
school. The word conjures up the image of a drafty
and rectilinear classroom, at the front of which stands
a teacher who is buttoned-up, pedantic, and (until
recently) male. Perhaps there is a chalkboard behind him
upon which he has diagrammed an English sentence by
clause and phrase; perhaps there is nothing but a voice
bellowing declensions of Latin nouns. Everywhere is
the threat of punishment. That threat may be explicit
or it may be implicit, but in any case it is credible, for
otherwise the students would not be filed row by row
and column by column. The antipathy for school is
bound up with its taste for DISCIPLINE: to punish, and
by punishing, to teach. That is how schools carry on
with the instruction of *artes*, or skills. Grammar schools
used to acquaint young aristocrats and sometimes their
bourgeois peers with the lingua franca; trade schools
reared the children of the poor into laborers, and often

members of a union too; now professional schools test a
college graduate for the capacity to master a swamping
volume of technical material, and they offer a license and
a network of colleagues to those who endure the ordeal
(see PROFESSION). But to trust the earliest sources in
the western canon is to see that it was not inevitable that
school should be punitive. Indeed the Greeks understood
school less as the means to an end than as the end itself.
Aristotle wrote in the *Nicomachean Ethics* that "happiness
is thought to depend on leisure (*scholē*)." The Stagirite,
unlike many who have reacted against him, believed that
school was an enclave for reflection and repose, and that
labor, such as levying taxes and waging war, involved tasks
undertaken precisely so that more time could be available
for contemplation (*theōria*). These two conceptions of
school—Augustine's, in which school is preparatory, and
Aristotle's, in which it is dilatory—pose a contradiction
that any serious inquiry into the matter must resolve. A
historical explanation for the opposition might point
out that the intellectual foundations of school as an
institution crumbled between the time of Aristotle
and that of Augustine—schools originally meant for
contemplation had become pragmatic (and punitively
so) by the end of the Roman Empire. There may be
another explanation, however—one suggesting that the
contradiction is built into school itself. Often it has been
observed that the children who hate school the most take
the longest to get through it. This perversity evidently
resonated with Augustine's generation as well, for he
wrote that "the process of learning with its attendant
punishment is so painful that children not infrequently
prefer to endure the punishments designed to compel

A
B
C
D
E
F
G
H
I
J
K
L
M
N
O
P
Q
R
S
T
U
V
W
X
Y
Z

them to learn, rather than to submit to the process of learning" (see IRONY). Indeed, as all teachers know, students will continue to endure such punishment *ad infinitum*, unless they fashion themselves into the pupils they were meant to be. In this way, students are caught in a double bind and suffer in either case. It thus becomes quite difficult to say what a rational student ought to do. The disquieting suggestion, in the end, is that school doesn't explain Hell so much as Hell explains school: "In fact is there anyone who, faced with the choice between death and a second childhood," Augustine asked, "would not shrink in dread from the latter prospect and elect to die?"

SCIENCE

The knowledge of a given phenomenon that has been acquired from study with a repeatable method or technique; also, often, the methods or techniques themselves (see METHODOLOGY). A bias in usage tends to reserve the term only for practices (and knowledge) insofar as these remain consensually veridical: old, bad, or wrong "science" tends not to be considered "science" in a satisfactory sense. Given that science has come to be conceived as a wholly progressive, accumulative, and auto-obsoleting enterprise, the unease about the scientific status of all past science leads to a number of paradoxes and obscurities (see PROGRESS). Science typically refers to knowledge that is positive, or fact-based, rather than normative, or value-based. Indeed, this conception is of such overwhelming importance that it may be no longer coherent to speak of value-based "knowledge" at all. In the middle ages, science spanned virtually every kind of inquiry then in existence, from grammar, rhetoric, and logic to arithmetic, music, geometry, and astronomy; in the Renaissance, it narrowed to something like "philosophy" (i.e., the set of principles or axioms from which one could deduce the foundation for inquiry into nature or culture); only in the Enlightenment did science begin to stand for empirical inquiry as such, especially that inquiry which is addressed to subsystems of discrete or pseudo-discrete natural phenomena (as in physics, chemistry, and biology) or cultural phenomena (as in politics and economics). Nevertheless, it was not until the middle of the twentieth century that science became modern (see KNOWLEDGE PRODUCTION). Under the watchful eye of the National Science Foundation, science has grown to military-industrial maturity. In order to

A
B
C
D
E
F
G
H
I
J
K
L
M
N
O
P
Q
R
S
T
U
V
W
X
Y
Z

understand why the NSF and the marketplace are so
entwined, one must consider the origins of the NSF itself.
It emerged from the Office of Scientific Research and
Development (1941–47), which mobilized scientists
(within and without the academy) for the production
of weapons during the Second World War. The OSRD's
chief triumph was an invention called the proximity fuse:
unlike earlier iterations of the same device, the proximity
fuse did not detonate upon colliding with the earth (the
contact fuse), or upon the expiration of an allotted time
(the timed fuse), but upon coming suitably close to its
target. Declassified documents attest that the efforts of
the OSRD were instrumental in the Battle of Britain.
With this newfound capacity to detonate explosives
in the mere vicinity of inflight objects, the vulnerable
coalition demonstrated advanced accuracy and lethality
in intercepting oncoming planes and rockets.

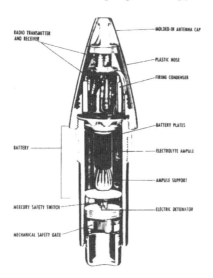

It was inevitable that the United States would marshal the extraordinary success of wartime invention and prioritize scientific research in the postwar period. Vannevar Bush, interwar director of the OSRD, was promoted president of the fledgling National Science Foundation in 1950; his chief objective was to design an agency that would be autonomous within the federal government. Bush's NSF would be unbeholden to the whims of a populace that suffered on occasion from bouts of anti-war sentiment: the prerogative of experts in fields like physics and chemistry (rather than lawmakers or voters), the NSF was for a time able to research the "pure" science that mattered so much to Bush. As proselytized in his plan, *Science—The Endless Frontier*, the NSF would promote "disinterest" in the name of scientific progress, and it would divide that project into three categories: basic research, applied research, and development. But because the NSF was decentralized, it encouraged competition for access to its considerable largesse. In order to win government contracts, businesses and universities had to build and maintain cutting-edge technology, hire the best scientists, and attract the brightest students. As Bush wrote in the preface to a history of the OSRD, "The contracting system which it developed [...] brought to being a pattern of administration which aptly met a new and unique need and which stands as a richly suggestive guide for other undertakings." And it was suggestive indeed: when college radicalism tested the will of the private and public sectors in the late 1960s and early 70s, it was the departments closely affiliated with the NSF (especially physics and chemistry) that sustained administrative ties

A
B
C
D
E
F
G
H
I
J
K
L
M
N
O
P
Q
R
S
T
U
V
W
X
Y
Z

to the military-industral complex; and when tax dollars vanished amid prolonged stagnation in the mid-70s, it was those same departments that proffered a template for the university to survive in the globalized economy. That template was simple: the NSF would approach university scientists with problems that emerged from the marketplace and subsidize their basic research in hopes that it would lead to applications that industrial labs and technology firms could monetize. Thanks to this private-public monopoly on scientific research, society enjoys superconductivity, optoelectronics, and deep-sea drilling. This successful "pattern of administration," however, was so successful that the NSF gradually dissolved into yet another organ of late capitalism. Max Weber believed that science was the vocation, peculiar to modernity, that did not know the meaning of the problems it set for itself. Weber's hypothesis still holds, with this exception: science no longer sets them.

SIGNIFICANCE

(*Current*) $p < \alpha$, where p is the probability of obtaining a result as extreme as, or more extreme than, the one actually observed, given that the null hypothesis, H_o, is true, and α is the arbitrarily chosen small probability of rejecting a true null. (*Archaic*) The meaning of a word or sentence, or the quality of bearing that meaning; the degree to which an object deserves study, attention, and care—its use to humankind.

A
B
C
D
E
F
G
H
I
J
K
L
M
N
O
P
Q
R
S
T
U
V
W
X
Y
Z

SUBJECT

Loosely, a body of knowledge or a topic of inquiry larger
or smaller than disciplinary or FIELD-level formations
(see DISCIPLINE). In reference to broad areas of study,
"subject" often occurs within the context of secondary
school education and applies to a non-professionalized
discursive register. Collectively, English, math, science,
and social studies represent a popular distribution of
various academic disciplines into subject areas in the
United States. A subject may also refer to an object of
scholarly study, however expansive (in the sense of a field)
or delimited (in the sense of a specific issue or theme).
In the latter regard, the subject occupies a local academic
setting as a subject of discussion or debate. There is no
lack of definitions for the subject in the sense of the
human individual. Synonyms, metonyms abound—and
complicate the resulting endeavor to extricate, if not
redeem, the individual from the tempest of critical
responses to metaphysical systems (see METAPHYSICS).
A shortlist of the overdetermined possibilities (the
rational subject, the Cartesian subject, the transcendental
subject, the autonomous subject, the speaking subject;
additionally: the self, ego, I, not-you, actor, agent, author,
speaker) embroils him/her (pronominal subjects) in a
lockstep of critiques—of Enlightenment, rationalism,
transcendentalism, ahistoricism, ideology, hegemony,
agency, autonomy, individualism, and humanism itself
(see CRITIQUE). Claim after counterclaim, however, the
subject remains; each metaphysical permutation attests
to its persistence. Subject. Is the subject the nucleus
of the HUMANITIES, the locus of humanistic inquiry,
the embodiment of "what it means to be human"? The
singularity of the subject undermines the synecdochic

arrangement whereby the part identifies the whole, the one stands in for the many, and the human individual incarnates the human community. The scholar does not exist in isolation from the group of peers who receive and evaluate his/her work. Scholarship presupposes audience: it culminates in an address, delivered by the subject as supplicant, to those with whom he/she presumes to identify. Yet even the academic plurality of subjecthood—the ostensible inclusivity (but recursivity?) of "we"—threatens the humility of humanistic inquiry. "*And how should I presume?*" Certain disciplines transfer objecthood onto the depersonalized "human subject" of research (generally scientific). Humanistic scholarship, in turn, encounters the human subject as object—perhaps inadvertently, and crossways, but persistently.

A
B
C
D
E
F
G
H
I
J
K
L
M
N
O
P
Q
R
S
T
U
V
W
X
Y
Z

SYMPOSIUM

An assembly of individuals contingently—or, in exceptional cases, essentially—persuaded that their conversation is more interesting and important than the thing they are in conversation about.

TEACHING

The gerundive of the verb "to teach"; also, as a
conventional substantive, "the material taught"—though
this usage is uncommon, and has come to convey a fusty
sententiousness, as in, "I am here to share with you the
teaching of a great sage." Teaching is generally understood
to involve the conveyance of information, methods,
skills, or perspectives *from* a person in possession of
same *to* a person substantially not so endowed. Thus
the activity implies the existence of "students," a general
term for individuals placing themselves (or having been
placed by others) on the receiving end of the teaching
act/undertaking/situation. One may, however, "teach
oneself" (see GRADUATE STUDENT). Within the
context of post-secondary education in the United States,
teaching is reliably defined as one of the three central
obligations of the professoriate, the other two being
research and service. It is explicitly upon these three
activities that faculty are evaluated (by their peers, as
well as by university administrators), and demonstrated
competence in these three arenas is treated as essential to
advancement. The exact status of teaching in this triune
context varies from institution to institution and from
field to field. Administrators of large universities tend
to make a broad distinction between teaching-intensive
disciplines (history, English, philosophy—though also
much of psychology, economics, etc.) and the sciences
(see SCIENCE). When such a typology is invoked, the
latter term refers not to an epistemically distinct domain
of activities (essentially all taught subjects within colleges
and universities having come to adhere to a relatively
homologous model of KNOWLEDGE PRODUCTION),
but rather to a subset of university departments in which

A
B
C
D
E
F
G
H
I
J
K
L
M
N
O
P
Q
R
S
T
U
V
W
X
Y
Z

the majority of faculty and graduate student labor is
supported by large-scale research grants originating in
government agencies, private foundations, and even
commercial entities. Faculty in such a DEPARTMENT
(paradigmatically physics, chemistry, biology, and the
related biomedical sciences) do teach (meaning they
enter classrooms and laboratories to assist undergraduates
in attaining progressively higher degrees of competence
in the relevant domain, doing so by means of lectures,
problem sets, discussion, and guided hands-on
investigation), but they tend, in the setting of research
universities, to do much less of it than their colleagues in
other departments (where external funding for research
and graduate students is much less readily available).
Teaching raises a number of challenging questions,
the (temporary/contested/contingent) resolution of
which effectively establishes the constitution of higher
education as such in any given time and place: What
should be taught? Who should teach it? To whom?
How? In practice, however, the rise of a nearly universal
conceptualization of knowledge as highly *progressive* (i.e.,
a commitment to the idea that domains of knowledge
properly change continuously, forever renewing their
form and content by means of internal dynamics that
cause new and better knowledge to replace older and less
good/powerful/useful/true knowledge [or even false
knowledge, a.k.a. *error*]) has tended to place *research*
(the pursuit of new and, therefore, notionally "better"
knowledge) in an ever more prominent position within
the culture of colleges and universities. Non-epistemic
factors have contributed to this development—not
least the discovery, during the Second World War, of

the enormous practical (military, economic) potential
of research in the sciences of matter, force, and life.
The resulting influx of resources for basic and applied
research in these areas into the institutions of higher
education in the post-war period necessitated new socio-
technical mechanisms for evaluation and assessment
(notably systematic PEER REVIEW) as well as new
administrative priorities and objectives. The status of
teaching in such settings saw revision, as did many of
the forms of academic life outside of the immediately
affected subject areas, in that the new socio-technical
and administrative mechanisms (together with the whole
model of research-driven academic life) gradually came
to play an increasingly prominent role across all academic
disciplines. It is possible that teaching is an activity
with stronger ties to self-formation than is commonly
acknowledged, and that in some disciplinary domains (or,
more generally, *outside* of specific disciplinary frames; see
INTERDISCIPLINARITY) teaching should be understood
as something other than the activity of conveying
information, methods, skills, etc., and even, perhaps, as
something inextricable from "soulcraft." But the notion,
whatever its virtue or appeal, is extremely difficult to
activate meaningfully, and tends to emerge almost
exclusively in reactionary and/or pathetic intellectual
settings.

A
B
C
D
E
F
G
H
I
J
K
L
M
N
O
P
Q
R
S
T
U
V
W
X
Y
Z

TEXT

That for which there is no outside. Myths, oral
legends, folktales, manuscripts, books, plays, paintings,
photographs, newspapers, magazines, advertisements,
LPs, films, television shows, radio programs, videogames,
social media profiles, blog posts, manifestos, viral threads
and/or web-based content, as well as all conceivable
objects, be they real or ideal, made, lost, or found,
terrestrial, celestial, or otherwise, may be "read" as "texts"
(see READING).

TRADITION

As heritage, a set of inter-generational practices and/or values that carry historical or genealogical significance. Disciplines cultivate tradition, be it manifested in a body of texts (see CANON), a way of thinking or knowing, or other valued objects or practices (e.g., so-called "smokers," or open cocktail parties at professional conferences). Assimilating such conventions allows scholars to invoke and engage their disciplinary traditions; failure to do so may place scholarly work outside a discipline's bounds. Tradition figures conceptually in Max Weber's "Science as a Vocation," which relates the progressive ethos of academic work to the antiquation of intellectual accomplishments continuously challenged, surpassed, and, as it were, demystified. Thus, tradition can be said to "evolve" as intellectual labor accumulates in the annals of a discipline—a process perhaps reminiscent of the act of discarding and/or forgetting itself. One's relationship to tradition evolves, often as a function of technological or political change. Contemporary access to resources, for example, has rendered academic labor simpler [sic]. It may be attributed to innovations such as Google and Wikipedia that encyclopedic schooling, as a tradition (e.g., "Great Books," "General Studies," etc.), has become largely outmoded. This consequence of PROGRESS *ad infinitum*—namely, the simplification of once laborious endeavors—raises questions over the value of disciplinary tradition. Among some disciplines, the inheritance of centuries past remains relevant, whereas, in others, relevant objects and interests are perpetually and scrupulously *au courant*.

UNIVERSITY

An autonomous degree-granting institution organized
around academic disciplines. The term, deriving from
the Latin substantive denoting the all-encompassing
totality of the universe as such, apparently came to
designate this circumscribed pedagogical entity without
IRONY. The university summons a community for the
disinterested pursuit of truth (though participation
in such communities involves, for some, paying large
sums of money; others, by contrast, are handsomely
remunerated). Elements of Enlightenment kitsch do
at times make appearances in the representation of this
enterprise as a whole: heroic and innovative scholars;
attentive and curious students; reasonable discussion
motivated by the prospect of consensus—or, in recent
years, inclusion. To the extent that the university
successfully advertises this image, it could be said
to conceal the elaborate bureaucracy—operated by
administrators, trustees, donors—that has quietly and
prudently transformed some of these institutions into
such lucrative enterprises that their status as non-profit
organizations has become a matter of legal dispute. There
may be said to exist a "high" and a "low" explanatory
narrative for the significant transformations undergone
by universities in the past century. The latter account,
while less easily assimilated to the university's ideals, may
well be more important to its past, present, and future, in
that it focuses on that sordid particularity that so often
gives the lie to utopian universality: cash money. As the
essential dynamic *explinans* within the low narrative
of university development, money (and the attendant
fiscal preoccupations associated with its presence or
absence) may adequately explain superstructural change

A
B
C
D
E
F
G
H
I
J
K
L
M
N
O
P
Q
R
S
T
U
V
W
X
Y
Z

that otherwise seems contingent or obscure. Examples might include an African American Studies program struggling for years to acquire departmental status, or the politics department reinventing itself as a pseudo-scientific institution pedaling rational choice analytics. On the one hand, such on-campus developments can be said to reveal something about academic trends, values, and discoveries. A look in the *other* hand, however, exposes a fistful of greenbacks being deployed in the promotion, management, and, crucially, the financing of these alterations. Within a university, departments must fight for a limited pool of funds based on the number of undergraduate students they attract and enroll. Also germane in this quiet tournament: the prestige of departmental faculty and, to a lesser extent, associated graduate students (insofar as the reputation of scholars— whatever the sharp limitations on their "fame"—redound to the universities that employ and produce them). Departments further compete for research funds made available on the basis of government interests and corporate needs, in that state and corporate entities ultimately earn and allocate the resources that support university construction and expansion. Such incentivized behavior in the "marketplace" of ideas surfaces the business realities of university life. And yet, universities do remain significant (potential?) sites of resistance to the increasingly pervasive incursion of market forces into every aspect of individual and collective existence. Which brings us to the aforementioned "high" narrative for university change. Stated succinctly, this account insists upon the pioneering role of universities in: 1) fostering progressive social change (gender equity, civil rights, healthcare innovations, etc.); 2) providing the principled theories grounding such developments; and 3) generating the positive knowledge (of both humans and nature) upon which (1) and (2) are predicated. It is possible to argue that many of the shifts seen in the organization of research and teaching within universities over the last century have proceeded from the exigencies attendant upon the pursuit of the goals above. That it is possible to make this argument, however, does not make it true.

A
B
C
D
E
F
G
H
I
J
K
L
M
N
O
P
Q
R
S
T
U
V
W
X
Y
Z

VOCATION

Within religion, God's calling of a disciple (see
DISCIPLINE) to a particular role in his/her spiritual
community; similar to, but not identical with, the secular
"career." Otherwise, the feeling of *being called* ("by
whom?" remains, in this case, an intractable question),
or the sense of being meant for a particular role in
one's (economic?) community. "Vocation" entails the
injunction to improve and apply what one is given, and
thereby conveys an unsubtle moralism. Although the
secular vocation exists in many forms, one regards it in
some connection to the professions (see PROFESSION).
Colleges and universities, the stewards of the professions
today, often bear responsibility for leading young
individuals to their respective vocations, and these
institutions work to develop students' interests and
capacities in an effort to prepare them for their future
lives. Of course, the pressure to discover a vocation can be
so intense that some students feel precipitated into hasty
or insufficiently informed decisions. This predicament is
perhaps attributable to the university itself, an institution
that has long since abandoned its original function of
training competent theologians (see THEOLOGY). In
default of that, the university addresses its residual sense
of obligation with help from the neoliberal marketplace
(alumni networks, on-campus recruiters, etc.) and the
psychological-counseling establishment. Still, one may
wonder about the authenticity of vocational anxiety,
given that the actual, experiential differences among
white collar jobs available to graduates of American
colleges and universities are, arguably, few. And in
the uncommon case that students select vocations
incomparable to those of investment bankers, lawyers,

or management consultants, the prospects for gainful employment are reliably dire. Those called to teach and serve within the university, for instance, likely embark on tumultuous vocational journeys that generally involve additional years of education spent honing specialized skills and developing effective professional habits, expertise, and pedigree (see GRADUATE STUDENT). Although this process of professionalization is beneficial in many ways, it also has notable drawbacks. Graduate school represents a time (and place) for legitimating professional expectations and, thereby, intellectual conformity; and this enhances competition, specialization, and disciplinary distinctions. Because the academic job market poses serious challenges in certain disciplines, graduate students with heterodox interests or inclinations toward interdisciplinary exploration yield to such temptations at their own risk. Many, indeed, repress their intellectual impulses to avoid marginalizing themselves or otherwise damaging their employment prospects. In sum, it can be said that the obligation to secure a paying job detracts from the best version of the intellectual or scholarly life—by, *inter alia*, jeopardizing intellectual curiosity and moral development, crippling creativity, and refiguring the high calling of delving the human as such into a sorry campaign to wrest a post-doc from one's beleaguered peers. Then again, it may be that the failure to find gainful employment is in fact the precondition for meaningful work.

A
B
C
D
E
F
G
H
I
J
K
L
M
N
O
P
Q
R
S
T
U
V
W
X
Y
Z

THEOLOGY

Historically, the singular discipline of university study. As late as the eighteenth century, it was conventional to regard theology as the "science" of the "divine." The university's stated mission to systematize the totality of knowledge according to the methods of semi-discrete "disciplines" at best partially conceals its appropriation of this pre-secular idiolect. The uncomfortable proximity is manifest in the physical location of today's theology "departments" (seminaries), which are typically adjacent to but institutionally autonomous from the universities that are their namesakes. To what extent the university encourages theological inquiry, even as an ironic transmutation of its founding purpose, is quite intentionally repressed. Nevertheless, it may not be unwarranted to speculate: instead of *progress toward understanding the infinite* (its original mandate), the modern university attempts *infinite progress toward understanding.*

A
B
C
D
E
F
G
H
I
J
K
L
M
N
O
P
Q
R
S
T
U
V
W
X
Y
Z